ETHICAL TOURISM:

WHO BENEFITS?

Institute of Ideas
Expanding the Boundaries of Public Debate

DEBATING MATTERS

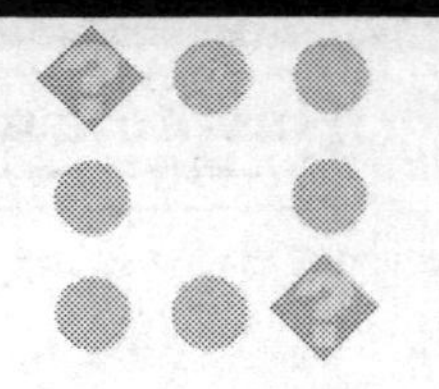

Institute of Ideas
Expanding the Boundaries of Public Debate

Tiffany Jenkins
Dea Birkett
Harold Goodwin
Paul Goldstein
Jim Butcher
Kirk Leech

Hodder & Stoughton
A MEMBER OF THE HODDER HEADLINE GROUP

DEBATING MATTERS

Orders: please contact Bookpoint Ltd, 130 Milton Park, Abingdon, Oxon OX14 4SB. Telephone: (44) 01235 827720. Fax: (44) 01235 400454. Lines are open from 9.00–6.00, Monday to Saturday, with a 24-hour message answering service. Email address: orders@bookpoint.co.uk

British Library Cataloguing in Publication Data
A catalogue record for this title is available from the British Library

ISBN 0 340 85734 X

First published 2002
Impression number 10 9 8 7 6 5 4 3 2 1
Year 2007 2006 2005 2004 2003 2002

Typeset by Transet Limited, Coventry, England
Printed in Great Britain for Hodder & Stoughton Educational, a division of Hodder Headline Plc, 338 Euston Road, London NW1 3BH by Cox & Wyman, Reading, Berks.

DEBATING MATTERS

CONTENTS

PREFACE

Since the summer of 2000, the Institute of Ideas (IoI) has organized a wide range of live debates, conferences and salons on issues of the day. The success of these events indicates a thirst for intelligent debate that goes beyond the headline or the sound-bite. The IoI was delighted to be approached by Hodder & Stoughton, with a proposal for a set of books modelled on this kind of debate. The *Debating Matters* series is the result and reflects the Institute's commitment to opening up discussions on issues which are often talked about in the public realm, but rarely interrogated outside of academia, government committee or specialist milieu. Each book comprises a set of essays, which address one of four themes: law, science, society and the arts and media.

Our aim is to avoid approaching questions in too black and white a way. Instead, in each book, essayists will give voice to the various sides of the debate on contentious contemporary issues, in a readable style. Sometimes approaches will overlap, but from different perspectives and some contributors may not take a 'for or against' stance, but simply present the evidence dispassionately.

Debating Matters dwells on key issues that have emerged as concerns over the last few years, but which represent more than short-lived fads. For example, anxieties about the problem of 'designer babies', discussed in one book in this series, have risen over the past decade. But further scientific developments in reproductive technology, accompanied by a widespread cultural distrust of the implications of these developments, means the debate about 'designer babies' is set to continue. Similarly, preoccupations with the weather may hit the news at times of flooding or extreme weather conditions, but the underlying concern about global warming and the idea that man's intervention into nature is causing the world harm, addressed in another book in the *Debating Matters* series, is an enduring theme in contemporary culture.

At the heart of the series is the recognition that in today's culture, debate is too frequently sidelined. So-called political correctness has ruled out too many issues as inappropriate for debate. The oft noted 'dumbing down' of culture and education has taken its toll on intelligent and challenging public discussion. In the House of Commons, and in politics more generally, exchanges of views are downgraded in favour of consensus and arguments over matters of principle are a rarity. In our universities, current relativist orthodoxy celebrates all views as equal as though there are no arguments to win. Whatever the cause, many in academia bemoan the loss of the vibrant contestation and robust refutation of ideas in seminars, lecture halls and research papers. Trends in the media have led to more 'reality TV', than TV debates about real issues and newspapers favour the personal column rather than the extended polemical essay. All these trends and more have had a chilling effect on debate.

But for society in general, and for individuals within it, the need for a robust intellectual approach to major issues of our day is essential. The *Debating Matters* series is one contribution to encouraging contest about ideas, so vital if we are to understand the world and play a part in shaping its future. You may not agree with all the essays in the *Debating Matters* series and you may not find all your questions answered or all your intellectual curiosity sated, but we hope you will find the essays stimulating, thought provoking and a spur to carrying on the debate long after you have closed the book.

Claire Fox, Director, Institute of Ideas

NOTES ON THE CONTRIBUTORS

Dea Birkett is a writer and broadcaster. Dea is author of *Serpent in Paradise* (Picador, 1998), a book about her journey to Pitcairn Island, which was shortlisted for the Thomas Cook Travel Book Award, and *Jella, From Lagos to Liverpool* (Gollancz, 1992), winner of the Somerset Maugham Award. She won a Winston Churchill Travel Fellowship to run away and join an Italian circus, where she worked as an elephant girl. She currently writes a weekly column on how to travel with children for the *Guardian*.

Jim Butcher lectures in the Department of Geography and Tourism at Canterbury Christ Church University College, specializing in the sociology of tourism and leisure. He is the author of *The Moralisation of Tourism* (Routledge, 2002) as well as a number of articles on modern tourism. Jim lives in Kent with his wife and two children, and when away from work, he enjoys guilt free holidays in Malta and France.

Paul Goldstein began his work in tourism as a lowly telex operator at an inbound company. The next nine years were spent at two large mainstream companies. He went on to become Sales and Marketing Manager at an Africa specialist in west London, and the last six years have been spent at adventure travel specialists Exodus. During his time in travel he has worked in Spain, France, the US and all over Africa. He has travelled to over 70 countries and is an award-winning photographer specializing in wildlife. Paul has travelled to sub-Saharan Africa over 50 times. While he is a very active traveller, it is the wildlife and wilderness that really attract him. He owns a small, tented camp in Kenya where his greatest joy is employing 14 local people. Most recently he has broken away from his beloved Africa and last month was photographing endangered tigers in India and then orang-utans in Borneo.

Harold Goodwin is Director of the International Centre for Responsible Tourism and co-founded Responsible Travel.com and the Responsible Tourism Partnership. He advised the Association of Independent Tour Operators (AITO) on the development of their responsible tourism guidelines. In 2002 he worked on a Department for International Development funded project with the South African Department of Environmental Affairs and Tourism on Responsible Tourism Guidelines for South Africa.

Tiffany Jenkins is Director of the arts programme at the Institute of Ideas. She is the commissioning editor of the society section of the *Debating Matters* book series.

Kirk Leech is a teacher, freelance journalist and broadcaster. For many years, his energies were devoted to revolutionary politics in the UK. Latterly, his interests have expanded to issues in the developing world. Having travelled and researched in Brazil, Ghana and India working with the International Educational NGO WORLDwrite, he is currently working on a paper and film on the consequences for local people of the construction of a sanctuary in Gujarat, India.

INTRODUCTION

Tiffany Jenkins

Where we go on holiday and what we do when we get there are subjects of animated argument. How to travel has become the focus for advice, regulation, rules and codes of conduct. Whether it is the demand that travellers boycott Burma, or the suggestion that they ask permission to take a photograph of a local, there have been many calls for holidaymakers to be 'responsible' or 'ethical', directed at everyone from a backpacker travelling for years or a package tourist on a one-week jaunt.

The case for responsible tourism now emerges from many sources, ranging from governments across the globe, to travel companies, Non-Governmental Organizations (NGOs), campaign groups, celebrities, and journalists. Two best selling books – Alex Garland's *The Beach* (Penguin, 1997) and William Sutcliffe's *Are you experienced?* (Penguin, 1998) – captured a popular and widespread mood that is critical of 'selfish' or 'self-indulgent' travellers and promoted the idea of taking more care about where you go and what you do when you get there. However, while there is a great deal of support for ethical tourism, there is disagreement about what it is and how it is best conducted; there is concern about the consequences of its impact; and some have profound reservations about the motivations behind the demand that travellers be ethical.

WHO ARGUES FOR ETHICAL TOURISM?

The commitment from governments across the globe to reforming the tourism industry was formalized through documents resulting from the 1992 UN Earth Summit in Rio, when 182 governments adopted Agenda 21. The first document of its kind to achieve international consensus, Agenda 21 asserted that travel and tourism should assist people in leading healthy and productive lives, in harmony with nature and culture. This document declared that travel and tourism: 'Should contribute to the conservation, protection and restoration of the Earth's ecosystem'; that 'Environmental protection should constitute an integral part of the tourism development process'; and that 'Tourism development should recognise and support the identity, culture and interests of indigenous peoples.' While the efficacy of Agenda 21 has been questioned, its recommendations have been widely supported.

On the policy agenda now are proposals for 'green' air taxes to be imposed on airlines by the European Union, in a bid to tackle climate change and to discourage people from flying. The fact that a powerful body like the European Union has proposed this kind of measure suggests that the tourism industry is considered a significant social problem, at the highest levels. The policy is a source of some disagreement. On the one hand it has advocates, such as environmental campaigner and journalist George Monbiot, who contends, 'flying across the Atlantic is as unacceptable, in terms of its impact on human well-being, as child abuse' (The *Guardian*, 29 July 1999). And on the other hand the Freedom to Fly coalition, an alliance of UK air users, businesses, trade unions, airports and airlines, has expressed some reservation about the effectiveness of the plans, suggesting restraint is not the answer. As they told me in April 2002:

> Any measure to encourage responsible tourism must prove itself effective in meeting aims, such as improved environmental performance or benefits to the local economy, without being outweighed by adverse effects such as loss of tourist income to local economies... The most effective answer to environmental problems in aviation will be through technological advance. Questions such as conservation of special nature sites and ensuring local economies benefit from tourism demand specific local responses.
>
> (Interview with editor)

The year 2002 has been billed as the year of Ecotourism, hosted by the World Tourism Organisation (WTO) and the United Nations Environment Programme. The UN headquarters' launch event involved the participation of several government ministers, heads of intergovernmental organizations and representatives of leading industry associations and non-governmental groups. In the UK, the Department for International Development pioneered 'Pro Poor' tourism in the developing world. Even Prince William, a possible future monarch, did his bit to be responsible when he took part in a project that included helping to build a wooden cabin in Peru.

Ethical tourism has its corporate side too. Many large firms have appointed a 'responsible tourism officer', such as travel companies Thompson's and British Airways. There has also been a dramatic growth in smaller companies offering more ethical holidays. The Association of Independent Tour Operators (AITO), which represents the smaller specialists of the travel industry, has focused on green issues since 1989, and has gradually encouraged similar interest on the part of its members, issuing its first Responsible Tourism Guidelines in 2001. Smaller travel companies are forthright about their emphasis on the responsibility of travellers and often claim journeys are more authentic this way. There are many NGOs involved in the promotion of ethical tourism, such as the World WildLife Fund for Nature (WWF), the Audubon Society and Conservation International. There are more specific projects such as The Gambia Experience or the Save Goa campaign and many others with specific smaller scale agendas.

Ethical holidays are certainly popular with the public and are promoted in the media. Popular television holiday programmes frequently urge the traveller to be considerate and discuss the impact visitors have on the host country.

Figures collected by The World Tourism Organization show that in 2000 world tourism grew by an estimated 7.4 per cent. The total number of international arrivals reached a record 699 million in 2000, according to results received by WTO through August 2001. Critics of tourism point to the rising travel figures as indicating a pressing need to encourage environmentally responsible travel, in particular highlighting concerns that aviation fuel contributes to global warming. Others argue that the rise of the global tourist is a very positive trend. The arrival of cheap airlines, such as Easyjet and Go, means that the less well-off and the young have greater opportunity to travel, and can therefore broaden their minds and experiences. Travel operator Pete Smith, for example, speaking in a debate at Standfords bookshop in London, emphasized the positive aspects of the expansion of travel by comparing the experience of his father who did not travel when he was young (it just was not done and was not financially practical) with the opportunities now available. Smith is an enthusiastic supporter of the freedom to travel now available to most young people and argues it is a great opportunity which all should relish and embrace.

ECOTOURISM – ARGUMENTS FOR AND AGAINST

The UN designated 2002 as the International Year of Ecotourism. The International Ecotourism Society (ICTS) defines ecotourism as 'Responsible travel to natural areas that conserves the environment and sustains the well-being of local people'. It has been described by the US organization, Nature Conservancy, as having the following elements:

- Conscientious, low-impact visitor behaviour;
- Sensitivity towards, and appreciation of, local cultures and biodiversity;
- Support for local conservation efforts;
- Sustainable benefits to local communities;
- Local participation in decision-making;
- Educational components for both the traveller and local communities.

(US Nature Conservancy, April 2002)

Klaus Toepfer, executive director of the UN's environment programme told The *Guardian* that ecotourism:

> Should provide an opportunity to develop tourism in ways that minimise the industry's negative impacts and actively promote the conservation of Earth's unique biodiversity. If handled properly, ecotourism can be a valuable tool for financing the protection of ecologically sensitive areas and the socioeconomic development of populations living in or close to them
>
> The *Guardian*, 9 March 2002

Ecotourism, he added, was 'far from being a fringe activity' and should not be regarded as 'a passing fad or a gimmick, or even as a secondary market niche, but rather as one of the trump cards of the tourist industry of the future'.

There are many critics of ecotourism. Some argue that it is a western agenda imposed on the host country regardless of what they wish for. For example, Sachs contends that ecotourists impose what they think is an 'authentic' experience on native peoples, who are forced to perform for them. This, he argues, is not only oppressive but perpetuates misunderstanding between these native peoples and western ecotourists (J. Sachs, *The Display of Culture: A Comparative Study of Eastern and Western Tourist Brochures*, 1993). Others take an equally critical but very different view. Jackie Alan Giuliano, writing for the Environment News Service, warns that ecotourism's efforts may just serve the interests of global corporations that are responsible for the destruction of tourist destinations in the first place. It allows the companies to appear ethical without really changing their behaviour.

POLITICAL RESPONSIBILITY

One of the highest profile ethical tourism campaigns was a UK government-backed boycott of Burma. In September 1998, Derek Fatchett, then a Foreign Office minister, wrote to the Association of British Travel Agents (ABTA), the Association of Independent Tour Operators (AITO), and the Federation of Tour Operators (FTO) to outline the Government's views on tourism in Burma:

> The Government wishes to draw attention to the views of Aung San Suu Kyi, and other pro-democracy leaders in Burma, that

> it is inappropriate for tourists to visit Burma at present. These leaders believe that foreign tourists visiting Burma do not help the development of democracy or human rights in the country.
>
> Letter to the Chairman of ABTA, Mr Keith Betton, 7 September 1998. Source: Foreign and Commonwealth Office).

The campaign to stop tourists going to Burma came to a head in June 2000 when Tourism Concern and Burma Campaign UK called on the publisher of the popular *Lonely Planet* country guides for travellers to withdraw its book on Burma. They refused to do so and argued that tourists could read the facts and decide for themselves. In their guide they outlined the pros and cons of travelling to the area concluding that: 'Tourism remains one of the only industries to which ordinary people have access. Any reduction in tourism automatically means a reduction in local income earning opportunities. For this reason alone, we continue to believe that the positives of travel to Myanmar outweigh the negatives', (*Lonely Planet* guide to Myanmar, Burma). Such debate about travel to Burma suggests that some ethical tourism advocates believe that concerns over the political situation in a country extend beyond safety issues for visitors in military dictatorships or zones of conflict, and extend to a duty on travellers not to visit countries that are guilty of human rights abuses or have undemocratic governments.

The discussion about ethical tourism has gained significant momentum in the last two decades. In the essays that follow, contributors situate their arguments against the background of the developments outlined above and present contrasting arguments about the reasons for ethical tourism, its consequences and its impact.

The first two essays discuss how travel has changed, and the authors put forward their arguments on whether the changes that have taken place are positive or negative. For travel writer and journalist Dea Birkett, who opens the discussion with a cultural examination of the way tourism has changed in the last 40 years, significant developments have taken place, but the advantages these changes are purported to bring are highly questionable. Once encouraged as an unquestionable good, Birkett indicates how tourism is currently under attack. She outlines just how extensive this change in attitude towards tourism is, but asserts that the main impact of this attack is to encourage all types of tourism to 'rebrand', in order to appear responsible and ethical. Rebranding is at best superficial but also, according to Birkett, carries with it a range of problematic assumptions about the differences between the developed and developing worlds.

Harold Goodwin, Director of the International Centre for Responsible Tourism at the University of Greenwich, also dwells on the changes in tourism. His reading of these changes leads Goodwin to draw a different conclusion to Birkett. Goodwin strongly makes the case for responsible travel. He argues that over the years tourism has created serious problems, and contends we need to address these immediately. Responsible travel is not simply an exercise in rebranding but a real development, Goodwin explains, and if tourism is conducted responsibly, the problems travel brings can be alleviated, and both travel destinations and travellers could benefit.

The last three essays focus directly on the issue of who benefits from responsible travel. Paul Goldstein, Sales Manager at the adventure travel specialists Exodus, agrees with Goodwin's argument that ethical tourism is necessary and beneficial. Goldstein rails against unethical tourists and unethical companies, contending that sustainable and ethical tourism is essential to the future of the developing world. Both tourist and the host country could and must benefit, maintains Goldstein. Tourists would get more out their holidays and, through their sustainable and ethical behaviour, the host country, both its environment and its people, would also see a marked, positive difference. In particular, Goldstein demands that the major players in the travel industry must shoulder a greater responsibility for changing travel than they do currently, and pressurizing them to do so is an urgent task. There is hope, Goldstein believes, but much more needs to be done.

This endorsement and support for ethical tourism is opposed in the final two essays that both look critically at the assumptions and consequences of ethical travel. Academic Jim Butcher looks at the changes in tourism with regard to the impact they have had for the tourist. He is concerned with the way travel has been moralized by advocates of responsible tourism. Butcher contends that there is a strong 'anti-people' attitude in the ethos of ethical tourism, evident in what he considers to be little more than a snobbish viewpoint that disparages holidays people take for fun and relaxation. Butcher maintains that this attitude undermines the experience of travel for many people: it hampers their experience, curtails a sense of adventure and sets up barriers between locals and the travellers. Tourists, he concludes, do not benefit from ethical tourism. Kirk Leech, on the basis of his research in several developing countries, takes an equally unfavourable view of the benefits of ethical tourism, from the perspective of the host country. Through the use of two case studies, he demonstrates how ethical tourism leads to the imposition of what he considers highly damaging changes on host countries from the outside – what he terms 'enforced primitivism' – to fulfil romanticized notions held by those from the industrialized world about local people and about nature. Leech argues strongly that the host countries do not benefit. On the contrary, ethical tourism overall constitutes a burden that hinders their progress and development. With ethical tourism, Leech asserts, the people of the host country have lost their autonomy and ability to make choices about how they live.

The essays in this book set out contrasting and passionately argued perspectives, which we hope readers will enjoy and find useful in drawing some conclusions about the role and responsibility of tourism, and about who, if anyone, benefits from ethical travel.

Essay One

RE-BRANDING THE TOURIST

Dea Birkett

One day, there will be no more tourists. There will be 'adventurers', 'fieldwork assistants' (with the voluntary organization Greenforce), 'exploraholics' (as customers of travel company Explore Worldwide), 'volunteers' (with environmental charity Earthwatch or private company i-to-i) and, of course, 'travellers' ('Absolute Africa attracts travellers rather than tourists' states the Absolute Africa Affordable Adventure Camping Safaris brochure, 2000–1). But the term 'tourist' will be extinct. There might still be those who quietly slip away to foreign lands for nothing other than pure pleasure, but it will be a secretive and frowned upon activity. No one will want to own up to being 'one of those'. It might even be illegal.

Already there are some who would like to punish people for going to certain areas of the world for their own enjoyment. Many groups, including Tourism Concern, call for the boycotting of Burma by tourists. The Burma Campaign UK is prepared, if their plea for an all-out boycott fails, to call upon the British Government to ban British passport holders from travelling there, much as American passport holders risked prosecution for travelling to Cuba. But even amongst groups who call for boycotts, there is little agreement about where we should avoid, and the list is constantly changing. In 2000, the Travel Writers Guild called upon its members not to accept press trips or commissions to write about Bali because of Indonesia's involvement in East Timor. Yet Tourism Concern (which would boycott Burma), in a recent issue of its newsletter *Tourism In Focus* (Winter 2001/2), carried an article entitled 'Counting on Tourists', by 'an environmentalist and owner of a herbalist shop in one of Bali's major tourist areas,' bemoaning the fact that, since 11 September 2001, there has been a severe downturn in the tourist trade to Muslim countries such as Indonesia.

Bali and Burma are only extreme cases in a trend to prohibit tourists from entering certain areas. Already, new countries are being added to the list of territories where we should fear to tread. Tourism Concern lists China, Botswana, Belize, Zanzibar, East Africa, Peru and Thailand as having areas that have all been adversely affected by tourism. Tourists only wreak havoc. Tourists only destroy the natural environment. Tourists only emasculate local cultures. Tourists bring with them nothing but their money. They must be stopped at any price. But how?

THE NEW FACE OF TOURISM

Less than 40 years ago, tourism was encouraged as an unquestionable good. With the arrival of package holidays and charter flights, tourism could at last be enjoyed by the masses. The United Nations declared 1967 International Year of the Tourist. A solution was passed recognizing tourism as 'a basic and most desirable human activity, deserving the praise and encouragement of all peoples and all governments.' By the 1980s, tourism was the largest and fastest-growing industry in the world. By the end of that decade, 20 million British people went abroad for their holidays.

It will not be easy to wipe out this massive, ever-growing tribe. Today there are over 700 million 'tourist arrivals' each year. The World

Tourism Organization (WTO) forecasts that, by the year 2020, there will be 1.56 billion tourists travelling at any one time. Even an event as seemingly damaging to the tourism industry as the 11 September attack on the World Trade Center does little to make a long-term dent in this increasing trend; it merely influences where the tourist travels. Now Africa is perceived as a relatively safe destination while the Caribbean, reliant largely on American trade and American airlines, is suffering a severe turndown. But soon it could be otherwise. Only the pattern of the movements change, not the overall number of them. The WTO is predicting annual growth rates of around five per cent. In the face of this, the challenge to forcibly curtail over a billion tourists from going where they want to go is immense. It is, in fact, so immense as to be impossible. You cannot make so many economically empowered people stop doing something they really want to do unless you argue that it is of such extreme damage to the welfare of the world that only the truly malicious, utterly selfish and totally irresponsible would ever even consider doing it. This is clearly absurd. Whatever benefits or otherwise accrue from tourism, it is not, despite what a tiny minority might say, in essence evil. It can cause harm. It can be morally neutral. And it can, occasionally, be a force of great good.

So the tourist is being attacked by more subtle methods than all out war. The tourist, like the Post Office (which temporarily became Consignia), is being re-branded in the hope it will not be recognized as the unattractive entity it once was. The word 'tourist' is being removed from anything that was once called a holiday, in the pamphlet that was once called a holiday brochure. So while there are fewer and fewer tourists, there are more and more adventurers and fieldwork assistants, exploraholics, volunteers and travellers. We will think these people are something different, doing something different from that which the tourist once did, whereas in fact it is some of the same people doing pretty much the same thing.

This re-branding of the tourist knows no boundaries. Everything surrounding it becomes infected with the same re-branding brush. (The mistake the Post Office made was to rename itself as a whole, without renaming any of its component parts. So a postman now works for Consignia, rather than for the Post Office, but the 'postman' part gives the game away. To be consistent, and to make us truly forget its antecedents, Consignia should have re-branded its postworkers, too.) So as soon as the tourist is re-branded, then the 'holiday' quickly has to follow. Adventurers, fieldwork assistants, exploraholics, volunteers and travellers do not go on holidays; that's what people who just want a couple of weeks a year escape from their everyday life and have a bit of fun do. Un-tourists (as I will call them from hereon) go on things called 'cultural experiences', 'expeditions' ('It's an expedition, not a holiday!' claims a Coral Cay Conservation Expeditions flyer), 'projects', 'mini-ventures' and, most tellingly, 'missions' ('The mission of any Coral Cay Conservation Volunteer is to help sustain livelihoods and alleviate poverty').

THE NEW MISSIONARIES?

The word mission is very apposite. While this re-branding is supposed to present a progressive, modernistic approach to travel, in fact it is firmly rooted in the Victorian experience (interestingly, the other word found commonly in un-tourism literature is 'discover', also reminiscent of the Victorian travellers' language. Un-tourists no more discover Africa and Asia than did the nineteenth-century explorers. Africans and Asians were there long before any of them). Like the Victorian travellers, the modern day un-tourist insists that the main motive behind their adventure is to help others (many Victorian explorers were missionaries and many missionaries were explorers, most notably, of course, David Livingstone). Whereas the mass tourist and the area they visit are anti-ethical and at loggerheads, the ethos of the un-tourist and the needs of the area they wander into are innately in tune with each other. Earthwatch assures that they will provide 'life-changing opportunities for you and the environment... See the world and give it a future.' Travel company Eco-resorts claims, 'Together, we can change the world, one journey at a time.' The very last thing on any of these modern-day missionaries' minds, when they write out that £1500 cheque for two weeks in Ecuador, is that they might be doing so in order to enjoy themselves.

The re-packaging of tourism as meaningful, self-sacrificing travel is liberating. It allows people to go to all sorts of places that would be ethically out of bounds to a regular tourist. Thus, un-tourists are free to travel to areas that are politically, environmentally and culturally vulnerable and sensitive, under the guise of 'mission'. Earthwatch's 'Cacti and Orchids of the Yucatan' biodiversity programme explains to would-be volunteers:

> The rare thorny plants populating the arid northern coast of the Yucatan are one of the most endangered ecosystems in Mexico. They are threatened because ... whole segments of coastal dune vegetation are being burned for livestock grazing, cleared for coconut plantations, or developed for *sprawling tourist resorts*. It is only a matter of time before the entire ecosystem collapses. You will be working ... to help reverse these troubling trends...' [my emphasis].

'Greenforce's 'Amazon Expedition', we are told,

> ... offers a rare opportunity to work in the most biologically diverse and seriously threatened region of the world. The

> Amazonian Rainforest is disappearing at a rate of two million hectares per year and yet this region plays a crucial role in the Earth's ecosystem. Our project in south-east Peru is working to further the quest for rainforest conservation and to uncover more of its infinite secrets...

In fact, the more threatened the area the more obliged the un-tourist is to go there on a mission to save it.

Ironically, these un-tourists go to the very same places from which many would have tourists banned. Indeed, this un-tourism relies upon exclusivity; it is all about preventing other people travelling in order that you might legitimize your own travels. Mass tourists are automatically, by definition, excluded from partaking of this new kind of un-tourism, as are package holiday goers. This latter exclusion is particularly self-deluding, as almost all of the new un-tourist travels – whether a safari, research programme or cultural exchange – are booked as a package. Many are extremely prescriptive of what you do when you get there, far more so than any major package holiday company would dare to be.

Pretending you are not doing something that you actually are – that is, going on holiday – is at the heart of the un-tourist endeavour. Every aspect of the experience has to be disguised. So gone are the glossy holiday brochures, those no-nonsense information providers mainly consisting of full frontal photos of each hotel, with flight dates and a room price stated clearly underneath. Instead, the expeditions, projects and adventures are advertised in a publication that is more likely to resemble a magazine with a concern in ecological or cultural issues. It is often not immediately apparent that they are advertising a holiday at all. The price, though steep, is usually well hidden, as if there is a reluctance to admit that this is, in essence, a commercial transaction that is being entered into, wherever the money is going and however it is distributed. There is something unedifying in having to pay to do good. It reminds me of when I wrote a newspaper article about 'Dinner Dating', a form of dating agency where you all go out to dinner in a small group with the woman who runs the agency acting as the host. There was instant mass delusion among the diners. They all pretended that they were at a regular dinner party, not that they had each paid £75 just for the privilege of being there in hope of finding a mate. One diner even asked me how I knew Hilly, the dating agency organizer. I knew Hilly, of course, through an ad she had placed in *Time Out* magazine for singles for her Dinner Dating agency. But I realized that was not the right answer. 'Friend of a friend,' I muttered, and the self-deception was complete. We all relaxed.

The various pamphlets, programmes and brochures disseminated by the un-tourist industry, are modelled on the advertisements produced by charities for their sponsored events, such as treks and bicycle marathons (some, but not all, of the companies offering un-tourist experiences are in fact set up as 'not-for-profit' organizations). The confusion between missionary work and vacationing is complete. The British Red Cross Trek Ethiopia 2002 brochure could, and maybe should, be regarded as an un-tourist experience. *Global Adventure* magazine produces an annual '99 Great Adventure booklet' which mixes sponsored events (for example, the Disabled Living Foundation's Mount Kenya Trek, or Colon Cancer Concern's Trek Vietnam) with commercial holidays (Exodus Travel's 'Thai Indo China Explorer' or Contiki Holidays' '4wd Outback Adventures'), as if there were no difference between them. Earthwatch is, in fact, a charity. Conservation charity BTCV now runs projects under the banner 'Go on Holiday – and Help Save the World!'

THE CONTRADICTORY IDEOLOGY OF UN-TOURISM

The central and simplest way to ensure that un-tourism retains its exclusive status is to limit the numbers who do it. Nearly all the packages are for small groups, rarely more than a dozen. Every un-tourist brochure guarantees that the expedition, safari, or project size will be strictly limited. This is justified on the grounds that it will minimize the impact on the environment and host culture. A dozen people, it is argued, will not do the damage that a whole coach-load would. But if there are limited resources – water, for example – surely any additional numbers puts an extra and unjustifiable strain on it? Or, if cultural contact is damaging, it is damaging however many times it occurs. One person is as likely to hand over a can of coke to an Amazonian Indian as two, 20 or 200 are. To say if you do something that has an ill effect a little less it will then have a good effect, is clearly nonsense; it will only have a little less ill effect. Un-tourists cannot claim that they are morally superior just because they damage the human and natural environment less than mass tourists; surely they must not damage it at all. According to their own reasoning, they are on a mission and must do good. Un-tourists are very concerned with appearing to hold the moral high ground. Afraid of being tainted by association, they avoid identifiably tourist infrastructures, such as hotels. (It is difficult, although not impossible, to be an un-tourist in the Canaries. Un-tourism concentrates on destinations in the developing world. Ironically, at the same time, the un-tourism industry condemns air travel as a pollutant, so how are we expected to get to Ecuador and Gambia?) They prefer to stay in a tent, a cabin, 'local-style houses' (yurts, thatched huts and so on) or, a typical example, 'a traditional Malay wooden stilt house.' ('Traditional' is presumed to be an uncomplicated, readily identifiable and innately positive quality.) These, they believe, are somehow more in keeping with something they call 'local culture'. 'Local culture' is very important to the un-tourist, whereas the mass tourist is believed to both shun and obliterate it.

Local culture, however, is often presumed to be place-specific. It is almost always applied to a culture of the developing world, and very rarely to developed countries. When in the developing world, we are encouraged to interact with the locals. On the Eco-resorts 'Women in Perspective Safari', Kenya, participants are taken to meet a women's self help group in the village of Nyeri. The i-to-i 'projects' include assisting 'a grassroots organization that uses various media to champion the cause of women and the disabled' in India. Kumika Expeditions caters to 'those adventurous travellers who want to experience first hand the local way of life.' Explore Worldwide describes its holidays as, 'An epic tale of discovery. Of small groups getting closer to a country's people and cultures, in 200 of the world's most unusual destinations.' Trips to meet hilltribes in northern Thailand, the 'tattoed Ifugua' of the Philippines, and 'ancient Berbers' in Morocco are common. When we travel to developed countries, however, 'the locals' are not deemed so attractive, and we are warned to avoid them. Rarely are we implored, when visiting New York, to check out a social housing project in the Bronx. In such a situation, 'cultural contact' is restricted to trading exchanges with store assistants, hotel porters, waiters and ticket booth salespeople. No one worries too much about that. But in the developing world, we have to seek out more meaningful contact.

As part of this meaningful contact, we are urged to 'respect local culture and customs'. What exactly does this mean? Again, it depends upon which area of the world you are talking about. The attitude towards the developed and developing world 'local culture' is very different. There are many practices that the English indulge in that the French, Americans or Spanish consider quite inappropriate, if not downright rude. However, we feel under no obligation to curtail our activities or attitudes when we holiday in any of their countries. We believe that they will understand that we are foreigners and that we are both different from them and ignorant of how things are in their country. We treat them as equals to ourselves – as tolerant or intolerant depending upon the individual person concerned. We do not see them as societies incapable of accepting behaviour, dress or strength or mode of language different from their own. We do not court nor do we expect their disapproval. We expect mutual respect.

In the developing world, we adopt very different attitudes. There, 'respect for local culture' is prefaced on a presumed innate inability within that culture to understand that there are other ways of living to their own. They are portrayed, in effect, as being perplexed by our newness. In addition, the developing world culture may be presented as oppressive, with the un-tourist at the vanguard of helping the local people throw of their shackles; back to the 'mission' again. And thirdly, local cultures in the Third World are presented as so weak and vulnerable that the arrival of a handful of western tourists (remember, we never travel in groups of more than a dozen) poses a huge threat. This is despite the fact that many of these cultures are more rooted, ancient and have survived far longer than any culture in the developed world. They are, in fact, examples of how very robust cultures can be. Most alarmingly, host cultures are portrayed as places with all three traits: incapable of understanding difference (so we must not alarm them), oppressive (often in how they treat women) and vulnerable (so we must be careful not to damage them). We are, without realizing it, conjuring up contradictory attributes – both weak and overpowering; intolerant, yet to be shown great tolerance. In practice, for the un-tourist 'respect for local culture and customs' means temporarily abandoning your own principles and beliefs, perhaps for no longer than a fortnight, in favour of your hosts', whatever their beliefs may be, and even if they are oppressive.

While tourism is considered to be at the very worst plain bad, and at the very best problematic for the developing world, it is often presumed to be an unabated good for the developed world. This difference in attitude towards developing and developed world travel was revealed most sharply with regard to tourism to the United States post 11 September 2001. Following the attack on the World Trade Center, appeals were sent out to tourists around the world that they should not abandon the city. Ground Zero itself even became a tourist site, seemingly with the approval of the citizens. There was no debate – tourism was seen in essence as a positive activity, as something that would contribute to the rebuilding of a shattered city. There was not a single voice of protest from the promoters of un-tourism, pointing out the negative aspects that tourism can have on a society. There was no discussion over how an influx of tourists might 'ruin' Manhattan. The environmental impact was not mentioned. It was presumed to be an unquestionable good for the local community, that they would benefit from tourism's revival and be harmed if it sank into further decline. But why? Because US culture is seen as somehow impregnable or less vulnerable to outside influences than other cultures? Despite its imperialist intentions, within its own borders the United States is extremely open to influences from outside. American culture is constantly changing and is very fluid. Generations of immigrants have defined and redefined what it means to be American. So why aren't tourists, with their different cultural influences and demands, seen as damaging to the essence of New York City – to its 'local culture and customs' – in the same way as they are to another culture? In trying to answer these questions, it becomes quickly apparent that the inconsistency highlights not differences between cultures, but differences in our attitudes towards them.

CONCLUSIONS

None of this ought to matter very much. Un-tourism makes up less than four per cent, in terms of expenditure, of the total tourism industry. The actual number of un-tourists is even smaller, as each one will spend more per capita than a regular tourist. However, they have been so successfully re-branded that they have come to define what it means to be a good tourist, that is, a respectful tourist, an eco tourist, and/or a responsible tourist. So what about the remaining 96 per cent of tourists – how do they, too, become un-? Or are we to abandon them, in their annual lager-soaked two weeks in the south of Spain? Are they beyond saving? Or can they, too, be shamed into being re-branded? We do not seem to care very much. Our efforts are almost exclusively centred on the upper edges of the holiday market. Tourists may survive in Europe much longer than they do in the rest of the world. Travellers, fieldwork assistants, volunteers, exploraholics and adventurers will go to Africa and Asia, and tourists will go to Italy and other European destinations. Tourism, a term which could once be applied worldwide, will, with the exception of a few popular places like Goa and Thai beach resorts, come to mean a geographically defined area of travel. In short, it will mean non-exotic.

It is easy to be prescriptive in a tiny part of the tourism industry. Matching 'responsible tourism' and 'mass market' is the challenge, as the Association of Independent Tour Operators (AITO) realises. Pointing to the often overlooked fact that many European holidays, such as gites in rural France, 'where holidaymakers meet the local people, live as part of the community and where their money benefits local businesses' are by their very nature 'green', AITO acknowledges that 'the standard charter-based package holiday requires much more determination in the search for green credentials'.

Yet in practice, it is in the area of mass-market tourism that the most meaningful, yet simple measures have been taken to curb the harmful side effects of tourism. Many hotel chains have made considerable efforts to reduce water consumption. While this does have the benefit of allowing a 600-bed concrete structure to brand itself as eco-friendly, it also does not demand that the tourist changes his or her spots. You are still allowed to be on holiday and have a good time, while showing consideration to the country that is hosting you. The only mission the holidaymaker is bound to is to get a suntan.

All tourism should be responsible towards and respectful of environmental and human resources. Some tourist developments, as well as inevitably individual tourists, have not been so and should be challenged. However, instead, a divide is being driven between those privileged, high paying, low in numbers tourists and the masses. They are doing exactly the same thing, but just being packaged as doing something different. Our concern, as AITO rightly pointed out, should be not with this small number of people, but with the vast majority of travellers.

But why should we bother? We who enter this debate are prime un-tourist fodder. We are not interested in saving leisure time abroad for the majority of the British people; we are interested in making ourselves feel good. That is why we have succumbed to the re-branding of our enjoyment and refuse to take up a term that we believe to be tainted. How many times have you willingly owned up to being a tourist? How many times have you preferred to use another label to describe yourself?

However, do we really want to be a 'volunteer' rather than go on holiday? Do you really want to be associated with the new missionary movement? Isn't it time to strike a blow against re-branding. Next time you are staying in that two-room local hotel in Oaxaca, reclaim a title that is rightfully yours. When asked by an adventurer, fieldwork assistant, exploraholic, or volunteer if you know where other travellers stay in Palenque, turn the classic rebuke on its head and say, 'I'm not a traveller; I'm a tourist.'

Essay Two

THE CASE FOR RESPONSIBLE TOURISM

Harold Goodwin

Since the first package holidays were organized by Thomas Cook in Victorian Britain, increasing numbers of people have participated each year in the annual pilgrimage to the sun, sand, sea and sex of the seaside resorts. Whether the destination is Blackpool, Minorca or The Gambia, holidaymakers seek their two weeks of hedonistic leisure in the sun. The annual holiday – and increasing numbers of UK citizens enjoy more than one holiday per year – is an opportunity for conspicuous consumption, a period of indulgence and of excess. As Angela Lambert has argued, '....people book holidays in order to make an outward and visible statement about their bank balance for the benefit of friends and fellow travellers' (The *Independent*, 3 August 1993). As we seek to escape from the rigours of work and other responsibilities we *let go*. Going on holiday is all about having a good time and leaving responsibility behind – or is it?

THE ECONOMIC IMPORTANCE OF TOURISM

Florida attracts very large numbers of domestic American and international visitors. David Bellamy has argued that 'Disney magic has created 45,000 well-paid jobs servicing the demands of millions of tourists' in an area previously degraded by the excesses of twentieth-century agriculture, and two-thirds of which is now a nature reserve (The *Observer*, 27 June 1999). Bellamy concludes that Walt Disney World in Florida is an example of good practice in responsible tourism; there are certainly significant conservation and economic benefits. Tourism is used to make the case for establishing national parks, creating new museums and heritage attractions, inscribing sites on the World Heritage List. The world's second largest industry is a major employer in London, Cape Town and Cyprus. Tourism has contributed to prosperity in Florida, Malta, Spain and a host of other destinations. Tourism has brought investment, jobs and a diversified economy to many – but not all – destinations. In some destinations market forces may reduce the rate of return on hotel lettings to the point where it is well nigh impossible to reinvest in the properties, the season may shorten to the point where the businesses in the destination cease to be viable and political events in the destination (or thousands of miles away) may undermine the industry and the livelihoods of local people. Tourism is not the only or necessarily the best route to development, but for many developing countries and post-industrial areas in the developed countries it is a viable option, sometimes the only viable option.

The United Nations Conference on Trade and Development has recognized that tourism can bring foreign exchange earnings, tax revenues, investment and jobs to the least developed countries (LDCs). The Canary Islands Declaration (March 2001) states boldly that international tourism is 'one of the few economic sectors through which LDCs have managed to increase their participation in the world economy. It can be an engine of employment creation, poverty alleviation, reduction of gender inequality and protection of the natural and cultural heritage'. The representative of the LDCs present at the conference recognized that most LDCs have 'significant comparative advantages ... conducive to viable tourism specialization'.

THE PROBLEMS OF TOURISM

Tourism Concern with their 'Our holidays, their homes' campaign has been arguing for some time that we should behave better than we do when away on holiday. Tourism necessarily involves travelling to other people's places to use their social, economic and natural environment. As Lord Marshall said at the British Airways Tourism for Tomorrow Awards in 1994, tourism and the travel industry '... is essentially the renting out for short-term lets, of other people's environments, whether that is a coastline, a city, a mountain range or a rainforest. These "products" must be kept fresh and unsullied not just for the next day, but for every tomorrow.' Lord Marshall's comments are widely cited for their endorsement of an enlightened self-interested commitment to maintaining the product unsullied, essential to the sustainability of the industry. The notion of short-term lets of other people's environments is potentially more radical. It raises the issue of who takes the rent and whether or not the rent is fair or sustainable.

Brian Wheeller has argued consistently that tourism development is accompanied by some negative impacts and that the trend is inexorably towards mass tourism. Wheeller argues that 'the sensitive traveller is the perpetrator of the global spread, the vanguard of the package tour' ('Tourism's Troubled Times', in L. Francis (ed.), *Sustainable Tourism*, Earthscan, 1997). He is right to conclude that economic benefit for local communities requires volume, and that sustainable tourism has indeed 'burdened itself with incompatible objectives – small-scale sensitivity and limited numbers to be achieved in tandem with economic viability and significant income and employment impacts.' Wheeller opines that 'irresponsible tourism' is a more accurate description, exploring progressive tourism but noting that the dictionary definition includes 'continuously increasing in severity and extent' ('Is progressive Tourism Appropriate?', *Tourism Management*, 1992). Arwel Jones has also argued that the social and cultural impact of independent travellers has been significant despite their small numbers, 'their values and behaviour reflecting more an outright rejection of Western capitalism than a respect for indigenous populations and social structures and traditions in countries such as India, Bali and Tibet.' He called for alternative approaches to tourism management and marketing that could be applied across the whole spectrum of tourism to achieve a 'more real and sustainable industry' ('Is there a real "alternative tourism"?', *Tourism Management*, 1992).

EXPLAINING MASS TOURISM

There is no quick fix for the problems created by tourism. Ecologists may argue that we should eschew the plane and motorcar in favour of walking and the bicycle. This is distinctly unattractive to most people and, even if it were not, would result in little alleviation of the problems caused by large numbers of people in relatively fragile natural and cultural environments. Tourism is a form of consumerism, a consequence of development and the transport revolution. As a mass consumer industry, it is a direct consequence of the increase in world population and a rise in the material standard of living, from which most of the world has benefited over the last two centuries. Domestic tourism is also growing rapidly in Brazil, China, India and South Africa. However, population growth and the increase in material wealth are inequitably distributed. Tourism reflects that distribution and is a minor contributory cause. When people argue that tourists should not go somewhere because they will spoil the place, we often mean that other people should not go there. It is those tourists who despoil the place; we travellers are different. Businessmen, research scientists, package holidaymakers, birdwatchers and gap-year adventure cyclists are all tourists. We all use the same facilities and contribute to the travel and tourism industry – it is in fact the case that today's adventure traveller is path-finding for tomorrow's tourist coaches.

Tourism is an experience, an opportunity to unwind, relax and be pampered or to test the body. For each of us it is a unique experience, a journey of discovery, an opportunity for enlightenment or excess. For many of us, tourism is a major expenditure, waited for, worked for, invested in, anticipated, it is our big purchase of the year and we expect the experience to see us through the rest of the working year. We have high expectations of that magical week or two in the sun or on the ski slopes. Tourism is also an industry, providing a livelihood for eight per cent of the world's work force with 200 million jobs in 1999, and 5.5 million new jobs a year in the first decade of the twenty-first century (World Travel and Tourism Council, *Millennium Vision*, WTTC, 1999). The travel and tourism industry may not be the world's biggest industry, but it is quite clearly a significant source of livelihood for a large part of the world's population, with annually increasing numbers of people taking domestic and international holidays in both the developed and developing world. Tourism is therefore both a leisure experience and a major industry in a large number of countries.

While for decades the main focus of debate has been on international tourism, there is increasing recognition of the significance of domestic tourism. As Ghimire has pointed out, between 1992 and 1996 domestic tourism grew by 13 per cent in Mexico, 23 per cent in South Africa, 30 per cent in Thailand, 31 per cent in China, 38 per cent in India and 39.5 per cent in Brazil (*The Native Tourist*, Earthscan, 2001). This represents a significant improvement in the material standard of living and the life experience of very significant numbers of people in the developing world. Ought we not to rejoice at this increase in equality?

WHAT IS RESPONSIBLE TOURISM?

The evidence is overwhelming that domestic and international tourism will continue to grow rapidly for the next several decades and, although the boom may not last forever, it would be irresponsible not to seek to manage tourism to make it more responsible. The naïve optimism of those who promoted forms of tourism that conformed with the exhortation to 'take only photographs, leave only footprints' is passing, and was already being questioned in 1994 by the notion of needing to pay rent for the use of other people's environments, as expressed by Lord Marshall. Tourism needs to be managed so that the triple bottom line – economic, social and environmental – objectives of the Earth Summit in 1992 can be realized. There is a marked trend towards responsible tourism, a wider concept than the environmental focus of the first five years after Rio. The tourism industry is being increasingly challenged to address the social and economic agenda of sustainable development.

Jost Krippendorf enjoined us to make a realistic assessment of our tourism role, recognizing that only if we succeeded in living with tourism as a mass phenomenon could we claim to be making a decisive step forward: 'After all, every individual tourist builds up or destroys human values while travelling.' Echoing the enjoinder 'global thinking – local action' Krippendorf asserts that, 'We must try to do it differently for once ... proposals must ... be as infectious as possible. Orders and prohibitions will not do the job – because it is not a bad conscience that we need to make progress but positive experience, not the feeling of compulsion but that of responsibility.' Krippendorf argues that our efforts to improve tourism 'must not degenerate into rules of regimentation and manipulation' but rather they must make possible 'the experience of freedom' (*The Holiday Makers*, Butterworth Heinemann, 1987).

REBELLIOUS TOURISTS AND REBELLIOUS LOCALS

Krippendorf seeks fair exchange and equal partnerships, relationships based on mutuality, equality and solidarity, a new and less exploitative form of tourism that should be measured by its capacity to contribute to 'gross national happiness' measured in terms of 'higher incomes, more satisfying jobs, social and cultural facilities, better housing ... Balanced tourism development must meet the interests of the host population and of travellers.' He argued passionately for a clear commitment to local culture and the celebration of local traditions in architecture, art, food and beverage. He felt that the world needed 'rebellious tourists and rebellious locals.'

Responsible Tourism is a movement – consumers, business people and locals seeking to harness the experience and the industry to make a better form or forms of tourism. Different groups will take responsibility differently and for different purposes, exercising their responsibility in a host of different ways; diversity is the very essence of human existence as well as an essential aspect of tourism and the concept of responsibility embraces it. Different consumers, companies and destination communities will aspire to realize their concept of a better form of tourism and take responsibility to achieve it.

RESPONSIBLE TOURISM CELEBRATES DIVERSITY

Responsible travel takes a variety of forms and can be characterized as travel and tourism that:

- Minimizes negative environmental, social and cultural impacts;
- Generates greater economic benefits for local people, and enhances the well-being of host communities by improving working conditions and access to the industry;
- Involves local people in decisions that affect their lives and life chances;
- Makes positive contributions to the conservation of natural and cultural heritage and to the maintenance of the world's diversity;
- Provides more enjoyable experiences for tourists through more meaningful connections with local people, and a greater understanding of local cultural and environmental issues;
- Is culturally sensitive and engenders respect between tourists and hosts.

(www.theinternationalcentreforresponsibletourism.org)

One of the most significant characteristics of the tourism industry is that the product is consumed at the factory, with the consumers (tourists) travelling to their chosen destination to experience the holiday they have purchased. From this stems their often negative, but potentially positive, environmental impact – the social impacts (positive and negative) of tourism and the economic opportunities. Tourists bring to destinations an additional market; they come with money to purchase sightseeing, fruit, meals, drinks, handicrafts, souvenirs and a host of other goods and services, potentially a significant contribution to the local economy. They are witness to the working conditions of the people who create their holiday, a vision that is potentially a force for good.

Harrison and Husbands argue that responsible tourism encompasses 'a framework and set of practices that chart a sensible course of action between the fuzziness of ecotourism and the well-known negative externalities associated with mass tourism.' Mass tourism they argue can be 'practised in ways to mitigate and obviate its obvious disbenefits' (*Practicing Responsible Tourism*, Wiley, 1996). Increasing numbers of operators are using the concept of responsible tourism to convey their approach to obviating these disbenefits and to improve the quality of their holidays. Harrison and Husbands argued that responsible tourism is 'a way of doing tourism planning, policy and development rather than a brand or type of tourism'. However, at the turn of the century increasing numbers of operators are placing their products in this category and new market interfaces such as www.responsibletravel.com are emerging and growing in popularity. Fundamental to the concept of responsible tourism is the assumption that all forms of tourism can be engaged in and organized in an increasingly responsible manner. Responsible tourism has sufficient breadth to be applicable to mass tourism operators and to specialist niche companies, and can be adopted by operators and by tourists. Yet responsible tourism is not an absolute – tourists and tour operators can be more or less responsible. Rather it is an aspiration that can be realized in different ways, in different originating markets and in the diverse destinations of the world.

Krippendorf argued in *The Holiday Makers*, that 'destination loyalty: travel more often, or even regularly, to the same place' should be valued. Only by revisiting destinations can 'we develop a true relationship to a country and its people.' Destination-loyal tourists are 'much more likely to feel that they must protect and embellish the holiday area.' Cynics may think this an idealistic approach, yet some idealism is necessary to set goals and seek social change. The Gambia is just one example of a popular revisited destination, although not a predominantly middle class one frequented by the chattering classes such as the cult status destinations of Tuscany or Provence. 'Busby Way' in the Senegambia Hotel is not named after Sir Matt Busby – it is named after a Mr and Mrs Busby who, in common with a number of other couples, have spent 25 or more holidays there. The Gambia is a special place for many European tourists who return year after year.

The Achilles' heel of responsible tourism is the necessity of travelling by air. A WWF report on the environmental impact of package holidays to the Mediterranean concluded that 70 per cent of the impact was caused by the emissions generated by flights to and from the destination. There are emerging campaigns around 'food miles' – the way food and drink travels thousands of miles before we eat and drink it – which reveals that this is an issue not only relevant to the tourism industry. Future Forests and Climate Care both offer mechanisms by which flyers can offset the carbon effects of their flights at a surprisingly low cost. Individual tourists, tour operators, airports and employers (for business travel) can all take responsibility for using and popularizing carbon-offset schemes. We can make a difference if we choose to.

WHOSE RESPONSIBILITY IS IT TO MAKE A DIFFERENCE?

Tourism is an industry and a set of experiences taken away from home; tourism is defined by the minimum of an overnight spent away from home. It necessarily requires a journey from home to a destination and, whether as a domestic or international tourist, the holiday experience is of someone else's home. Individual consumers and the tour operators, marketing and PR agencies and agents who shape travellers' choices and offer their products can all make more or less responsible choices. As consumers we should be looking critically at the media which inform our choices – travel journalists and writers, guide book writers and publishers, advertisers and programme makers – and ask ourselves whose purposes are they serving? Are they part of the problem or part of the solution? Ecotourism failed because it was devalued and became no more than green-wash. Responsible tourism requires that all of us – holidaymakers, tour operators, developers, hoteliers, agents, attractions, airlines, guides, coach operators and car hire companies – declare what responsibility we are actively taking to make tourism better for the environment, for local communities in destinations and for holidaymakers.

A MOVEMENT FOR RESPONSIBLE TOURISM

Writing *The Holiday Makers* in 1987 Krippendorf felt that the turning point would come 'when informed tourists take to the road and simply demand a re-orientation of commercial policies.' He began the campaign for tourists to become critical consumers, mature tourists seeking 'not to exploit but to assume responsibility.' Tourism Concern has campaigned for many years using the 'Our Holidays, Their Homes' slogan. A Swedish NGO in Slovenia campaigned using the slogan 'Your everyday life is their adventure.' As Lord Marshall asserted back in 1994, all travel and tourism is about the short-term lets of other peoples' environments.

As consumers we make choices about how we enter into those lets. We make choices about how we behave in the destinations, other people's homes. The VSO WorldWise campaign in the late 1990s asked tourists whether they would meet any local people, challenged them to get more out of their holiday, asked whether they would go shopping in a supermarket at home wearing only a swimsuit and pointed out that many people travel to the most distant locations on earth and never eat, drink or shop outside their hotel. They advised '... if you look for it there's probably a market just down the road – you can buy direct from the crafts-people and see local traditions come alive. An experience for you. A livelihood for local people. Just ask.'

The WorldWise campaign focused on encouraging people to have better, more enjoyable holidays, with the strap line 'How to get more from your holiday'. Responsible holidays are real holidays. As Justin Francis of responsibletravel.com argues, responsible travel will over time, like organic food, become a mainstream consumer favourite, better for the consumer and better for the planet and local people. Fair Trade coffee and tea have been consumer success stories, consumers feel good when they consume them but they do not taste different – responsible holidays are better experiences.

The movement for responsible tourism is gathering pace – we can make tourism a better experience for hosts and guests. Valene Smith's aspirational usage of the language of hosts and guests (*Hosts and Guests the Anthropology of Tourism*, University of Pennsylvania Press, 1989) offers a more egalitarian, more humane way of thinking about tourism and a means of escaping the superficial experience of most package holidaymakers, independent travellers and backpackers. What is for the visitor a unique experience is for the tourist industry worker or local person living with the impact of tourism, a monotonous, routine and often irritating experience. Many of us want better holidays. We need to make choices which will achieve that aspiration.

CONSUMER TRENDS

There is increasing evidence that the movement for more responsible forms of travel and tourism is beginning to impact on mainstream consumer preferences. There is still a long way to go but progress has been made. ABTA, the Association of British Travel Agents, conducts an annual survey of consumer opinion about travel. Their September 2000 survey found that for 29 per cent of holidaymakers the reputation of the holiday company on environmental issues was very important, with a further 41 per cent saying that it was important. Thirty-three per cent said that the provision of social and environmental information in tour operators' brochures was very important to them, rising to 78 per cent if we include those who regard this information as fairly important. For 85 per cent of respondents it is very or fairly important that their holiday does not damage the environment, and for 77 per cent that it should include visits to experience local culture and foods. For 71 per cent of holidaymakers it is very or fairly important that their holiday benefits the people of the destination to which they are travelling, for example through jobs and business opportunities.

In the same ABTA survey, 45 per cent of holidaymakers said that they would be prepared to pay more for their holiday if the money went to preserving the local environment and reversing some of the negative effects of tourism. Interestingly, this is the same percentage that reported in the same survey that they regularly recycle glass at home. Fifty-three per cent said that they would pay more for their holiday if workers in the destination were guaranteed good wages and working conditions. Seventy-seven per cent of respondents to ABTA's survey reported that they would be prepared to pay an extra £10 or more on a £500 holiday. Whether or not customers would pay extra for these 'benefits' is a moot point, but the significant point is that they have aspirations to do so. Travellers look for trips which offer the destinations and activities that they seek, with availability and price as the next major determinants of choice. However, tour operator competition includes elements of responsible tourism in the construction of the product and, for mainstream products, responsible tourism elements are part of the competitive offer. ABTA's figures suggest that these elements will be relevant to consumer choice where destination or activity, price and availability criteria are met.

Tearfund, one of the UK's leading Christian relief and development agencies, has conducted surveys of consumer attitudes towards ethical or responsible tourism in 1999 and 2001. In autumn 2001, 52 per cent of consumers said that they would be more likely to book a holiday with a company that had a written code to guarantee good working conditions, protect the environment and support charities in the tourist destination, that is a seven per cent increase in two years (Tearfund, 'World's Apart', 2002). Sixty-five per cent of consumers would like to know more about how they might support the local economy, preserve the environment and gain information on local customs, politics and religious beliefs so that they can behave more responsibly when they go on holiday. That is an increase of two per cent in two years. Twenty per cent of respondents said that they would like to receive an information sheet with ten tips for ethically responsible tourism.

REAL HOLIDAYS

Tearfund promotes a code for tourists, which enjoins them to make the most of their holidays:

Make the most of your holidays...

1. **Find out about your destination** – take some time before you go to read about the cultural, social and political background of the place and people you are visiting.
2. **Go equipped with basic words and phrases in the local language** – this may open up opportunities for you to meet people who live there.
3. **Buy locally made goods and use locally provided services wherever possible** – your support is often vital to local people.
4. **Pay a fair price for the goods or services you buy** – if you haggle for the lowest price your bargain may be at someone else's expense.
5. **Be sensitive to the local culture** – dress and act in a way that respects local beliefs and customs, particularly at religious sites.
6. **Ask permission before taking photographs of individuals or of people's homes** – and remember that you may be expected to pay for the privilege.
7. **Avoid conspicuous displays of wealth** – this can accentuate the gap between rich and poor and distance you from the cultures you came to experience.
8. **Make no promises to local people that you can't keep** – be realistic about what you will do when you return home.
9. **Minimize your environmental impact** – keep to footpaths and marked routes, don't remove any of the natural habitat and reduce the packaging you bring.
10. **Slow down to enjoy the differences** – you'll be back with the familiar soon enough.

... **And ensure that others can too**.

www.tearfund.org

Many other groups and tour operators are developing similar codes for tourists and travellers. In the age of consumerism, consumers have real power; with consumer pressure, competition can begin to drive responsibility. Fair Trade, non-animal tested cosmetics, organic foods and responsible tourism are all examples of market-led social change where social businesses have been active.

RESPONSIBLE TOUR OPERATORS

VSO's WorldWise campaign reported on tour operators' travel advice to their customers and concluded that they were travelling in the dark. If tourists were to have better holidays and to manage their impacts to minimize the negative and accentuate the positive, they needed better information. In 1999 this seemed a radical demand, yet some progress has since been made, with the advice now more complete and more responsible than it was (VSO, 'Travelling in the Dark', 1999 and Tearfund, 'Tourism, putting ethics into practice', 2001). A number of tour operators and the Association of Independent Tour Operators (AITO) responded to the campaigning and AITO now have an explicit commitment to responsible tourism practices. Companies are making clear commitments about what they regard as responsible about their practice. They will be judged on their performance by clients and by the media. Companies adopt responsible practices for a range of reasons: personal commitment, awareness of the importance of corporate social responsibility and, of course, for commercial advantage. Some operators now identify a responsible ethos as central to their strategy to ensure repeat bookings. Members of www.responsibletravel.com fulfil clear minimum criteria before they join that market place, but it is the specific claims made by individual companies and for particular trips, which excite consumer interest and drive best practice. As Justin Francis argues, fairly traded tea and coffee do not taste different, but a responsible holiday should be different, offering a more enjoyable holiday, a better and more fulfilling experience. It is clear that the responsible tourism practices of operators are not usually the primary determinant of consumer choice – activity or destination, availability and price are generally far more important – but non-price competition among operators around responsible tourism is shaping the market place.

Many of the lessons of the failure of the concept of ecotourism in the originating market countries have been learned. Ecotourism was always a tiny niche, while responsible tourism is applicable to the mainstream of the industry. All companies and individuals can be more or less responsible about their impacts. Over time everyone can become more responsible, particularly if competition drives the industry in that direction. Ecotourism quickly degenerated into green-wash. Responsible tourism requires that people are specific about their claims. The claims can then be challenged and false claims fall foul of trading standards legislation. Ecotourism quickly lost its marketing power; there was little product differentiation or diversity. Take a look at www.responsibletravel.com to see the wealth of travel experiences available. A responsible travel approach celebrates diversity – there are many different ways in which we can choose to be responsible and to make positive impacts. Responsible travel rejects the lowest common denominator approach of many labelling schemes.

RESPONSIBLE TOURISM IN DESTINATIONS

Responsible tourism is no panacea. Planning for responsible tourism cannot be limited to the impacts of individual enterprises – it is the cumulative whole that needs to be addressed. Destinations are beginning to attempt to manage the impact of tourism in destinations to accentuate positive impacts and minimize negative ones. The emphasis is shifting from numerical headlines based on national arrivals and foreign exchange earnings, towards the sustainable management of specific local destinations with a particular focus on minimizing environmental impacts and maximizing economic benefits to local communities. The linkage between tourism and poverty elimination has been emphasized by the aid agencies (the British Government's Department for International Development, www.propoortourism.org.uk and UN Commission on Trade and Development) and by the World Tourism Organization and the World Travel and Tourism Council. South Africa has adopted national guidelines for responsible tourism and each sector of the tourism industry is now articulating its approach.

CONCLUSION – WE CAN ALL MAKE A DIFFERENCE

Brian Wheeller argues that responsible tourism is a 'so-called solution that keeps almost everybody happy', appeasing the guilt of the thinking-tourist while providing the holiday experience that they, and we, seek. It is an 'ephemeral and inadequate escape route' for those 'unable, or unwilling, to appreciate or accept their/our destructive contribution to the international maelstrom,' he claims ('Tourism's Troubled Times', in L. France, *Sustainable Tourism*, 1997). Scepticism is appropriate and the claims made by operators need to be scrutinized. However, in a world where sustainability is still a long way beyond our grasp it is irresponsible to reject 'win–win' scenarios because they are not total and complete solutions.

One can hope, Canute-like, that the World Tourism Organization forecasts are wrong and that international tourist arrivals will not reach 1.6 billion by 2020. As more and more people secure the income and leisure to travel we can reasonably expect very significant growth in international and domestic tourism. We need to learn to manage it. Better to do some things that are identifiable, specific and measurable, than to do nothing to minimize the negative and maximize the positive impacts of the tourism industry. As the Asian aphorism has it: 'Tourism is like fire. You can cook your supper with it, but it can also burn your house down'.

Tourism numbers are not likely to be significantly reduced by consumer angst about individual impacts. We may feel concerned about the impacts of tourists, but we are a long way from recognizing that we – travellers and tourists – are part of the problem. We are more likely to become part of the solution if we can consume holidays and travel in ways that minimize negative impacts and maximize positive ones. Canute-like we can rail against the evils of tourism but that will not make for a better world. The progressive alternative is to exercise our individual and corporate responsibility as consumers and enterprises, and to empower local authorities in destinations to manage tourism. We take 'Our Holidays in Their Homes,' we should respect and empower our hosts – they can only be empowered collectively. We may have cleaner hands if we stand aside from the practice of responsible tourism, but we will not make the world a better place. We must take responsibility and begin to make the changes – we can constructively criticize those who are not changing fast enough but reward and encourage those who are making progress. Be a critical consumer – take a real holiday.

Essay Three

CAN WE CARE ENOUGH?

Paul Goldstein

'The raw material of the tourist industry is the flesh and blood of people and their cultures.'

Cecil Rajendra, Human Rights activist, Malaysia

Mallorca, Angelo's Bar, June: Caucasian holidaymaker, dressed as only the British can, demands, 'Paco, dos cervesa por favor' before turning to his fellow drinker smirking. 'This Spanish lingo is pretty easy eh?'

Serengeti, Tanzania, January, migration time: Eight minibuses corral a lone female cheetah, interrupting her hunt. The 40 biped predators had their fill at lunch and their dinner is assured. Hers is not, and she and her cubs will now have to look elsewhere for theirs, or go hungry.

Mumbai, India, March, street scene among the slums: Photographer catches the moment as a weeping child cries out for food and stretches out imploring hands just as a passer by brushes her aside, framing her misery perfectly with his flowing robes.

La Paz, Bolivia, May: After an hour of haggling and bartering with some desperate 1980s t-shirts a tourist finally secures a bargain price of $15.00 for an alpaca sweater.

Nungwi, Zanzibar: Sunbathing Italian tourist anoints her naked breasts with another coating of uber-tanning oil.

Dominican Republic, Caribbean: Tourist spends $20.00 at the gift shop of his all-inclusive beach hotel, killing time before the transfer for his flight home.

Fleet Street, London: Journalist puts finishing touches to grammatically correct 500-word article on violent Tamil Tiger incursion in northern Sri Lanka.

Lhasa, Tibet: Passenger hurries to join up with tour group before entering the Potala Palace.

All of these examples are common occurrences, all thoughtless, and all display a total lack of respect or even awareness of local needs and susceptibilities – put simply, they are ethically bankrupt. Somehow these, and thousands more such daily incidents, must be curbed otherwise the world's tourism birthright will be completely compromised. The key question is stark in its simplicity 'Do we care about the countries we travel to?' If the answer will be 'not much', then the consequences for global tourism are bleak and the 'sea, sand, sex, cheap booze and bargain shopping' ethos will swamp even those precious enclaves of sanity that remain for the concerned and appreciative traveller and bring blight and degradation to as-yet unexploited regions.

The problems are transparent. The solutions are difficult, complex and in many cases long-term and does every one involved – tourists, travel agents, tour operators, hotel groups, airlines, national tourist boards – have the patience and commitment to act before it is too late? This is a crucial question. Put in facile terms, what are tourists bringing with them, what do they leave and what do they take away?

THE BIRTH OF RESPONSIBLE TOURISM

About 30 years ago the first overland vehicles, normally ex-army trucks, started trundling across Europe and beyond reaching far off iconic bastions such as Afghanistan, Nepal and India. For many this was a cheap and adventurous way of discovering lands that the few mainstream travel companies left well alone. This was their very attraction and although that market has diminished over the years, there is still that yen to travel in this style simmering within many people. These early expeditions did not trail blaze, nor did they pollute the areas for future travellers; they were a novel way of travelling and suited both traveller and host country alike. The developing world realized the opportunities offered by this style of travel and as the number of tourists increased so did the opportunities for local people to benefit. Sadly these promising early days were not a benchmark for the future. The advent of cheaper and more frequent air travel, as well as a greater range of the new planes, meant that a world still in its infancy of travel was about to be subjected to the potentially disastrous advent of a demanding but ill-educated public.

It took until the early 1990s for a tourism conscience to develop and, in a few rare instances, be dusted off. Unfortunately the big companies, the multiples, mainstream travel wholesalers who disgorge millions of passengers on unsuspecting indigenous populations, soon weakened the hands of numerous countries with burgeoning tourist markets. In many instances they have imposed brutal commercial 'values' on areas ill-equipped to 'benefit' and the effect has been detrimental. In others any benefits have been minimal, and what is particularly galling is that through a mixture of poor information and ignorance, the majority of passengers finish their holidays without a thought of how they could benefit their hosts. There is no ill will involved, merely heedlessness and apathy.

What have the majority of tourists brought with them? Tragic clothes, Ambre Solaire and duty free booze. What have they left? Very little since their money has usually been paid up-front to international chains or that greatest leech of tourism today – the all-inclusive hotel. What do they take away? A peeling suntan, blurred happy snaps, a runny tummy and a miasma of knowledge of the country they have visited.

At about the same time the loathsome skin trade lost its appeal, a small band of often ex-travellers founded travel companies that started giving broader and more sympathetic views on foreign countries, challenging the myopic outlook of the mainstream wholesalers. The former companies clearly do care where they are going, sadly only a very few can take sufficient numbers to really make an impact on global travel in the developing world. Despite often describing themselves as 'eco' companies, they do not own a permanent camp on the moral high ground. Frequently they are hobby organizations fulfilling the nomadic desires of wealthy dilettante directors or more venally just offering a quick fix to a social conscience. Yes, they are important. Yes, they can make a difference. But generally they are not catering to an unweaned public but to those well versed in responsible travel.

'Eco' is prime spin phraseology. A sympathetic sound merely providing a nebulous title to a somewhat murkier end result. During the early 1990s two particularly cloying 'eco' phrases permeated the travel ether:

Be a traveller not a tourist

Take only photographs, leave only footprints

Both are classic examples of mellifluous word play. They slake a demand for social travel identity, but in real terms are as patronizing as they are damaging. We can designate ourselves with whatever protective nomenclature or moniker we desire, but on leaving our own domicile, without holding long-term visas, we are all by definition tourists. It is the correct, honest description of most of us who travel 'abroad'.

The second mantra of photographs and footprints is slick and sinister. This smooth phrase is loaded with good intentions but short-changed by a spineless true meaning. If wanting to leave something, leave money, the hard variety and lots of it as this, more than anything, can make the fundamental difference to local people's lives. They ideally have to be made aware of the importance and value of tourism in their area and the most appreciated way is by remuneration. In the cases where visitors and companies are made palpably unwelcome this should be respected. The worst example of this is where tourism takes upon itself the ideological mission to 'protect' native communities while actually hindering their progression. This is not to decry all charity organizations for both the poor and for wildlife in these countries but a personal visit and donation carries far more gravitas. In many instances there are stumbling blocks to any sort of reward percolating down in the developing world, a world beset by bureaucracy and corruption, but they should not be used as excuses.

In dismissing the term 'ecotourism' it is important to explain the critique. This empty phrase is a knee-jerk reaction to guilt at intruding on the developing world and has no end product. *Sustainable, ethical* and *responsible tourism* are the keys to the advantageous future of these areas, and a wide cast of players have major roles to play in what is a complicated, emotive and long-term equation as I outline below.

TOURISTS

Access to global travel has never been easier. Travel booking is light years from where it was even ten years ago. Despite the recent demise of many dot.com companies – all hype and no substance – many people are booking holidays direct through computer-linked communications, often with little or no idea of exactly where they are headed, or what they can expect from the local lifestyle. It is a situation that bodes ill for those at their destination. Travellers to the developing world can be divided broadly into three categories: (a) mainstream (b) backpackers (including organizations such as Operation Raleigh) and (c) small group travellers.

MAINSTREAM TRAVELLERS

This is the category that can really make a difference with millions of passengers from the UK alone visiting the developing world each year. Current favourite destinations served frequently by charters are the Dominican Republic, Brazil, Kenya, Tanzania, Sri Lanka and The Gambia. In each of these local people can benefit whether they be beach vendors, local bar and restaurant owners, taxi drivers and boat operators, temple guardians or game wardens. The principal problem is that a large majority of passengers are incubated in their hotel units to such an extent that they seldom leave the perimeters. Some might 'bravely' venture out to squeeze off a photo of an impoverished fisherman not thinking for a moment that this might be both intrusive and offensive.

It goes further than this: tourists can leave indelible marks on the landscape which are obscured by unscrupulous international companies. The much maligned Anita Roddick of Body Shop remarks, 'The more you travel, the more you see there's a dark side to tourism and I don't see tour operators being dedicated to clearing up the mess. Cultures are invaded and food, languages, coral reefs and land disappear.'

Tourists and travel operators are inextricably linked. Without integrity on both sides, but especially without education, there is likely to be little change.

BACKPACKERS

Backpackers can bring a great deal to local communities. Sadly this is not always the case. Backpackers often have much more time than regular tourists but generally not a wallet full of money. In his hysterical book, *Are You Experienced?*, William Sutcliffe gives a brutal dissection of the very worst type of backpacker in India. His view is not fiction. The type of young traveller described appears to have bags of attitude and chutzpah while actually they are doing little more than trawling from one travellers' hovel to another with a *Lonely Planet* guide hanging from their back pocket. They deceive themselves that they are immersing themselves in local culture, while scrounging hospitality from those whose poverty is as great as their pride in welcoming the stranger – 'the locals were *so* friendly.' Some countries are making strenuous efforts to close any available doors to hordes of backpackers. Bhutan is pursuing a carefully rationed policy of promoting tourism in a manner appropriate to local climate and a hefty levy is payable just to enter the country, hopefully not misappropriated (another story). So, backpackers go to Nepal instead where they eschew anything remotely organized and try as ever to get everything on the cheap, while convincing themselves that they occupy the moral peaks.

Typical of the more abrasive side of backpacking is the story of two girls stranded in India who hitched a lift with a truck driver who charged them ten rupees (about 15p each). Before leaving, one of them riffled through the guidebook and trumpeted that the fee should be five rupees and that they were being cheated – try that on a London minicab driver for a touch of colourful invective.

As places become popular they are included in various guidebooks which regrettably can influence things irrevocably for years to come. The books say little about the people, just how to get there, where to stay and eat and the sightseeing attractions. Tourists then complain because the listed prices do not take into account that time passes and things change and frequently fight with shopkeepers and hotels over tariffs. An odious sub-culture can develop where the intention is not to meet the people and encounter the culture but vie with fellow travellers about who can travel the most and spend the least – a competitive sport that is as irksome as it is insensitive.

Like the *true* ski-bum – doing any sort of job just to get on the slopes – there are thousands of big-hearted backpackers who are both sympathetic and generous, not necessarily with money but with time and compassion and interacting with their hosts. They frequent local guest houses, bars and restaurants and use public transport which all generate income for the community. Their main reliance on guidebooks is to find out where *not* to stay. These people shoulder the burden of responsible tourism almost by default, acting as goodwill ambassadors to erase the impression of Westerners that many of their contemporaries have besmirched.

SMALL GROUP TRAVELLERS

Although by no means saints, these travellers offer more hope than their counterparts. Many are intimidated by 'going it alone' and join a group for reassurance and companionship. The guides with them are frequently local and used to dealing with group numbers of between eight and 16, not 40 to 59 cosseted in air-conditioned coaches. Much of the joy of travel for this individual is in the type of transport and accommodation with no time for bland international hotels. A stay in a longhouse, rondavel or a yurt is something to be treasured and the success of a holiday can also be gauged by a rickshaw, canoe or third-class sleeper journey. They bring more to the party, though they maybe not be well groomed, and are welcomed by their hosts.

When the overland scene was reaching its zenith in southern Africa in the 1990s, a number of grand local lodges and South African travellers very publicly criticized this breed of traveller. After a year or so of this, the local tourist authorities worked out that actually a truck full of 18 travellers was much more lucrative for them than a few toffs staying in $500 a night eight-room lodges. The 'despised' travellers paid with hard currency and into the hands of those who needed it most.

TRAVEL OPERATORS

In many cases the antichrist travel operators are perpetrators of some of the greatest ethical tourism stagnation in years. It is an unpalatable irony that as travel operators they could be offering so much to local economies in terms of sustainability but invariably leave the host countries short-changed. This broad heading of organizers can be divided into retailers, mainstream wholesalers and group travel organizers.

RETAILERS

Many retailers are vertically integrated with their wholesaler and have very different priorities from even 20 years ago, and since 11 September 2001 there has been heavy consolidation. Even ten years ago the principle ingredient in their harsh business plan was to satisfy accountants and their shareholders. That, tied in with the drive for 'market share', resulted in the perfect recipe for ethical catastrophe. Because of cut-throat competition and an overabundance of retail outlets, as well as many more people booking online, the word service was unofficially retired. What retailers are invariably selling is a discount, £400 holidays churned out with 15 per cent off at least, giving a margin of a few pounds per person travelling. This has not gone too far to be arrested but until service is restored, big business ideals will hold both the passenger and the smaller, more individual retailer to ransom. Their staff are poorly paid and the perks are not what they were, but the British public will never sacrifice its holidays, so despite the harbingers of doom saying otherwise the majority will still be booking through an agent ten years down the line.

The specialist companies will survive as there are plenty of small ones who have not crossed the Rubicon in terms of discounting and service, as will a handful of the multiples (the others will be discounted into oblivion) but, the small chain or independents will face increasingly difficult challenges, not made easier by airline commissions becoming more miserly.

As well as being better educated themselves in terms of ethical tourism, retailers must be better informed regarding their client base. A recent Tearfund survey found 65 per cent of passengers would like to know from travel agents and operators how to support the local economy, preserve the environment and behave responsibly when they go on holiday. Over half said they would more likely book a holiday with a company that had a written code to guarantee good working conditions and protect the environment. This encouraging statistic is still staggeringly ignored.

THE MAINSTREAM WHOLESALERS

Most, but not all wholesalers, are purely profit driven. There was a hint of conscience a few years ago when the inside cover of a 300-page brochure *did* refer to their purported care for the environment. It also sported green emblems from various eco societies and crowed that they contributed a sum to the poor and needy for each passenger who travelled. This is cant. It amounted to about a pound a head and there was rarely accountability. As companies grew increasingly answerable to shareholders, even these small concessions dried up and they are now conspicuous only by their absence. This is symbolic of their whole outlook.

There have been cries of outrage from restaurants to eco-environmentalists and from small hoteliers to beach vendors but their muscle-wielding power is too weak to alter the status quo. The Dominican Republic used to be a small, poor Caribbean Island. It is still a small, poor island except that now it can accept 747 jets. Planes fly and disgorge their passengers in a manner similar to the huge floating hotels, mysteriously classified as ships, that cruise around the calmer waters of the world giving passengers a few pre-arranged hours on each island visited, their bed nights being tightly ensconced on board.

The vast majority of hotels in the Dominican Republic are all-inclusive enclaves in keeping with much of the Caribbean now.

Passengers are collected by hotel buses, go on organized hotel excursions and barely ever leave their hotels independently. Nor need they spend a penny of hard or even weak currency when they are there. They pay up-front, and the inclusive concept is sold as a convenience package with little regard for its implications. International chains like Superclubs and Sandals benefit enormously, but the slice of pie left over for the local people is a meagre one. This is reprehensible on almost every level.

There are many insidious examples of this selfish, self-centred form of inclusive accommodation:

- In St Lucia aggrieved local merchants, restaurants, bars and shops urged the Government to introduce a two per cent levy on all all-inclusive passengers to help balance their books. The Government were in favour but refused due to pressure imposed on them by the all powerful all-inclusive companies.
- In Gambia foreign tour operators opposed the Government's ban on all-inclusive resorts, even though 99 per cent of Gambians involved in tourism were in favour and the Sunwing Hotel has actually closed because of the ban. This sounds like a victory for the residents, but think again. The ban is about to be lifted.
- In Mexico in 1989 the Government moved the people of Huatulco on the Cancun Peninsula to make way for development. Marina Garcia, previously a store owner, writes 'My village was right on the beach and had 500 families, it doesn't exist any more. Now we own a souvenir shop and a craft stall, some months we make enough to get by at other times we don't even make enough to pay the £80.00 monthly shop rent.'

There are many other examples of residents being denied access to 'public' beaches, or in Jamaica being illegally charged to enjoy their coastline. Discounting, market share, convenience selling and a lack of publicized alternatives all add to a pernicious sub-culture which proliferates each year offering little hope for the local people and their environment. The biggest crime of all is thinking that passengers will not pay a bit extra for a more ethically sound holiday. They will, but unfortunately no large operator feels it can justify taking such a quantum leap. After all is there any *real* pressure on them, apart from local residents and ethical tourism organizations? No, nor is there likely to be.

GROUP TRAVEL ORGANIZERS

This is a step in the right direction, but the alarming forecast is that many will not survive since they do not fly sufficient numbers to benefit from competitive airfares. With 'market share' and other marketing dogma such as 'diversity' and 'customer care management', as well as controversial 'new' money being infused into this growing area of travel, their future is doubly uncertain and their demise would be a loss to the whole industry. What they do well is take groups of passengers to far-flung developing areas of the world, prepared with a sympathetic eye and hard currency to spend. They utilize local guides and backwater attractions, as many backpackers do.

None of them includes cash-rich companies, and all are increasingly driven by the demands of accountants, the tyranny of the bottom line and the injection of that Trojan Horse, 'venture capital'. The latter, in particular, alters the soul of a company and respected and adhered principles frequently become compromised and, shortly afterwards, expendable. It is not all gloom since there are many ethically sound small companies with responsible attitudes to travel but is this enough to negate the above? They work with local staff, use sustainable principles and genuinely care about the many countries to which they send customers. It is low-impact tourism with a high-impact reward, the very opposite of mainstream companies.

Discounting holidays has become part of the travel calendar and they benefit no one – least of all the misguided consumer who frequently gets short changed in terms of standards and quality. With the short haul market, albeit the developed world geographically, it has gone too far to be arrested, but a possible solution to the ethical and financial nonsense of discounting could take the form of the following:

1. Stop all discounting to the developing world.
2. Make this annulment very public.
3. The money that would have been lost on discounting is given to sustainable tourism charities in the developing world.

Travel to these areas may account only for a small percentage of all destinations but the publicity would be huge, passengers would 'buy' into this ethical exercise and the company will lose nothing financially as the money was going to be discounted anyway.

GROUND OPERATORS

As far as ethical tourism is judged, the ground handlers have as much a moral imperative as the international wholesalers. They are literally 'on the ground' determining which hotels, guesthouses, bus companies and so on are used and, despite huge pressures from operators which can result in cost cutting and poor service, they have a major role to play. In some countries they are tightly controlled by the governments.

Tibet

Here China is replacing local tourist guides with ethnic Chinese staff, since it cannot tolerate Tibetan guides talking to Western tourists about the country's political situation. This is just one example of the ethical outrages and immoral acts regularly perpetrated by China as the occupying power. The Dalai Lama, barred from his homeland, implores travellers to keep visiting Tibet, but endeavour to use Tibetan-run tourist facilities. At present only two international companies worldwide run their own vehicles in China/Tibet, passengers being able to see what they want to, not what the Chinese authorities instruct them to.

Cuba

The image holiday companies conjure up of Cuba is of azure oceans, clouds of aromatic cigar smoke and thumping rhythms of the samba and salsa. This is quite true, since this is all most travellers experience from their regimented units at Varadero. The average citizen can buy only basic necessities with local currency, so a Cuban dance teacher needs to attract and teach tourist students all week for about $100. But this is not easy says Damian Diaz, a 33-year-old teacher. 'If I am in public with a dance student police will often stop me and ask to see my ID because they suspect I'm a hustler. Even if I could afford to eat in the tourist areas or visit their beaches, I could not. Cubans are barred from these places.' This is not only a hotel problem, it is also a problem with governments, as discussed below. Some of these restrictions on Cuban nationals are Castro's doing.

AIRLINES

Can they help? Yes, easily. Once they pioneer yet another route into the developing world they suddenly obtain great power over that country and its people. They should work closer with local governments and tourist offices, but more importantly with the local people to ensure the passengers unloaded can bring benefit to the population, not just the airline's bottom line. Passengers' anxiety about travelling in poorer areas of the world could be assuaged by an airline that shows a heightened awareness of issues surrounding tourism in developing countries. BA's 'Change for Good' appeal, collecting passenger's loose change to fund local charitable work, is a start but a company's ethical policy must be swallowed whole, and digested, by everyone from directors to staff before their considerable influence can be properly harnessed.

TOURIST BOARDS / GOVERNMENTS

In the developing world the two are incestuously entwined. Tourist boards are funded, or under-funded, by the governments and rely entirely on this money to project a favourable impression to their market.

The image of a country is paramount, so it is essential to have a good tourist board to promote this through overt publicity. Being competent in the arena of damage limitation is also crucial in the event of a disaster. Currently the tourist boards serving the UK are largely useless, with a few exceptions that include Hong Kong, New Zealand, Thailand, Australia, South Africa and most of the Europeans. The rest are poorly staffed and savagely under-funded. Their governments are at fault here, venally eager for tourist dollars yet whinge when the going gets tough. The monies that governments rake in are vast, yet benefits to both the local economy and indeed travellers are sparse.

Kenya

With the biggest income in East Africa from tourism why does this country have the worst roads? What happens to the $50.00 visa fee each tourist pays before leaving home? The 'money-today' attitude is incredibly damaging and the lack of foresight is hindering real development. When incorruptible politicians do become involved, such as Richard Leakey, foreign aid is ramped up and the benefit is apparent to all, in his case for tourism, local people and wildlife.

Uganda

Local issues also contain a moral imperative. In the early days of HIV/AIDS President Museveni embarked on a nationwide education programme and let the world know it. His is the only country in Africa, though still high, with a decreasing rate of the disease.

South Africa

Mr Mbeki's lunatic platitudes over the origins of HIV, in defiance of all medical opinion, have led to widespread condemnation from the media and health workers alike and have done little to maintain faith in his country in the post-Mandela era. It is possible to have the best tourist board on earth, but if your own government is falling down it will compromise all positive activities.

Brazil

For years there was no UK representation, so when people thought of Brazil they thought football, death squads, muggings and slums of *favellas*, all culled from the tabloids. The outlook is different now.

Mauritius

Pressure does sometimes have an effect. Recently the Ministry of the Environment blocked proposals for a new hotel being built in the Blue Bay marine national park, saying the eco-system is too fragile and the risk of marine pollution is too high. It was a rare success, for too often these concerns are overlooked.

Zanzibar

But for intense pressure from the UK organization Tourism Concern, a $4 billion construction would be underway on the northern end of the island with golf course, airport and luxury hotels. The original plan had blatantly failed to mention the peninsula's 20,000 residents who had had no say in the decision and were scared of being kicked out of their homes as the Mexicans were in Cancun. The Government had not lifted a finger to help, keen not to neuter their reward in this monstrous blot on one of the world's most beautiful coastlines. A delicate coral reef was threatened as were fishermen and farmers' livelihoods as well as guesthouses and small hotels, to say nothing of human rights.

These are the murky surfaces of tourist development that the promotional billboards do not want outsiders to see. In collusion with frequently unprincipled governments they find it all too easy to ride roughshod over any claims to infringement of human rights. A well-funded, honestly run tourist office, dispensing accurate information, backed by a sympathetic government is critical in the sustainable success of long-term tourism in the developing world.

THE MEDIA

Press, television and radio are absolutely crucial with their ability to shatter a country's tourism potential with one rabid headline or hyperbolic report. Bad news is good news for editors and their advertisers so it is far easier to rubbish a country than praise it and damage done in minutes can take years to correct. There is a moral obligation to report *accurately*, not in broad generalizations.

'Earthquake in Turkey', renders the entire Black Sea area dangerous. A girl is murdered in Malawi so the whole of East and Southern Africa is written off. South Africa is palpably more dangerous now than 15 years ago yet the politically correct coverage of any atrocities there is played down. Even travel publications are little better, giving scant lip-service to ethical tourism. Quite recently in a patronizing glossary on The Gambia, under a 'What's hot and what's not' banner, the latter contained the questionable advice that 'On leaving the hotel tourists may be intimidated by the poverty they see.'

Politicians do little to help, despite prating of democratic rights. Zimbabwe is crying out for justice, yet its neighbours prevaricate and Commonwealth members fudge the issue of expulsion. Prime Minister Tony Blair added little weight to the crisis a month before the crucial March elections by visiting *West* Africa – about as far away from the trouble spot as possible and his platitudes appeared all the more disingenuous by the fact that diamonds and oil are up for grabs there to say nothing of arms sales.

Current coverage on holiday programmes is controlled by the audience rating figures, and hence the bland mainstream fare on offer. A superb Michael Palin programme is no more than armchair stuff being so esoteric in terms of those who would emulate his travels to be no help to those countries he has visited. Mainstream programmes are boring, predictable and verging on patronizing, doing little for small countries or poor ones, but boosting the major companies' bottom line. Until television coverage becomes more ambitious, audiences will be forced to sit through another Judith/Juliet/John or Shanka eating yet another ice-cream, on yet another sun-lounger beside yet another heated swimming pool. The recent appalling practice of parachuting B-list celebrities into the developing world does little for their future. The *Survivor* series, whilst undeniably mainstream viewing, has brought scant reward to its host to say nothing of the more lasting physical effects of their tenure.

It seems to be unrealistic to expect people planning their holidays to do extensive research on their destinations so they tend to rely on 'expert' advice. The Foreign Office website, that oracle of government, would have them believe that Syria, Iran, Sri Lanka, Sudan, Ethiopia and Uganda are countries best avoided no matter what. In fact, these countries probably have the most hospitable and friendliest people on earth and desperately want normal contact with the rest of the world.

There are also more basic environmental problems associated with tourism:

1. In the mountains the increase in trekking activities can cause drainage and sewage problems, path erosion and disturbance of animal and plant life.
2. Cruise ships, unless well-maintained and self-contained, can cause contamination leading to health hazards to local people and destruction of aquatic plants through discharge of sewage.
3. Hotel and golf resorts, as well as eliminating plant and wildlife habitats, can also erode beaches and cliffs and destroy geological features. They are also profligate with water.
4. Increased demand for water from all holiday developments often means shortages in peak season and, typically, it is the local community who suffers.

These are simple obvious examples but are seldom heeded by tourist development companies.

CONCLUSION

Time to review those introductory examples:

Mallorca, Angelo's Bar: Ethical tourism is not just for the developing world. Parroting a few basic words and then pretending to have an unerring grasp of the native lingo is ignorant and rude. Take the trouble to learn it properly and see how people respond positively to your genuine efforts.

Serengeti, Tanzania, migration time: Read up on the area and wildlife before leaving home. Once there listen to the advice of guides and drivers and don't offer money to 'get in closer'. Respect whose back yard you are in, both man and beast.

Mumbai, India: There is nothing picturesque about poverty to the poor, so how much is that photo helping that hungry child? Take it if you must, and if possible get a name and address to send it to, but be sure to reward the individual immediately.

La Paz, Bolivia: Just because it is a developing country, currency does not suddenly become less valuable. How much is $15.00 to the haggler? Very little, but the vendor may be desperate to sell to gain a livelihood, so pay a fair price.

Nungwi, Zanzibar: In a Muslim country respect custom and tradition, or travel where such nudity does not cause offence. A little education and consideration goes a long way in the developing world.

Dominican Republic, Caribbean: Try at least to buy items in the local shops or markets where it will bring some benefit to local traders.

Fleet Street, London. News is news, but those 500 words may be disastrous for that county's tourism. Most people's geography is extremely hazy and potential tourists are easily alarmed, so specify the exact small region concerned and do not overdo the scare stories.

Lhasa, Tibet: Choose your travel company carefully, most are tacit supporters of an undemocratic, despotic government.

There is hope, but it needs nurturing. If a more ethical approach to *all* tourism is widely ignored, as it is now, then that hope will be extinguished and an ethical critical mass will be breached. The major players in the industry must shoulder a far greater responsibility than they do now for ethical tourism and not leave it to the smaller companies to carry the torch on their own. They in turn must not be let down by their governments. It is no use having expensive Earth Summits in Rio (2001) and South Africa (2002) if column inches are the only gain. Direct action must ensue and quickly.

Tourism is a business, but it should not be a carve-up of assets and profits with the international conglomerates, their directors and shareholders pocketing the lion's share from mega-developments with little benefit accruing to the host countries. Some of our favourite new destinations are also among the most impoverished on the globe. India, Nepal, Peru and Mexico are countries where millions survive on less than a pound a day, they rely heavily on tourism and it can bring many benefits. Sadly, too often it brings negative effects or the benefits simply bypass local people.

Travel companies and airlines as well as governments, tourist boards and the press must surely learn that the only way to ensure long-term profits is to co-operate with these host countries, listen to their concerns, consider not just the financial implications of new projects, but be sensitive to the local needs of those affected. If this is done ethically both parties can benefit.

Essay Four

WEIGHED DOWN BY ETHICAL BAGGAGE

Jim Butcher

Tourism has traditionally been associated with carefree relaxation, adventure and hedonism. For generations of people, holidays have offered a chance to escape the rigors of work and, perhaps, also the moral regulations laid down by family and community. However, today our holidays are subject to critical examination by the growing ethical tourism lobby, who cite natural and cultural barriers to our desire to travel for leisure.

In place of traditional package holidays, ethical advocates propose a range of alternatives – ecotourism, community tourism, cultural tourism and green tourism to name a few – all of which prescribe a big dose of nature and proscribe crowds, resorts, frivolity and fun. They advocate a new school of tourism in which we are encouraged to reflect on our supposed role in damaging the environments we visit and in diluting the culture of our hosts. The once innocent holiday is guilty until proven ethical.

I will argue that ethical tourism is a barely concealed slight on the 'unethical' package holidaymaker. It is an attack on the average tourist. The plethora of ethical advice diminishes the very things that *make* holidays – fun is frowned upon and a sense of adventure reigned in by the ethical advocates. And if this were not bad enough, the advice assumes that tourists and hosts cannot get on. It ends up reinforcing differences and creating misunderstanding.

ETHICS VERSUS THE MASSES

From 50 million international leisure travellers in the 1950s to some 800 million today, tourism has grown enormously (although it is worth noting that this represents only around 15 per cent of the world's population). The growth of tourism has created greater opportunities to travel to sun-soaked sandy beaches, snow-capped mountains and the cities of the world purely for leisure. This is something to celebrate, surely?

Not for the advocates of ethical tourism. For them the package holiday revolution is characterized by environmental destruction and fraught cultural encounters. An industry that brought the possibility to travel for leisure to millions is frequently viewed through a dark lens and caricatured as the harbinger of 'concrete jungles', 'lager louts' and cultural levelling. Rather than being cause for celebration, the figures quoted above are cited as evidence that tourism has gone too far too fast. The supposed scale of the problem created by the growth of mass tourism is summed up by Jonathan Croall in his apocalyptically titled book *Preserve or Destroy – Tourism and the Environment* (1995):

> Over the last 30 years or more mass tourism has had the effect of ruining landscapes, destroying communities, diverting scarce resources, polluting the air and water, trivialising cultures, creating uniformity, and generally contributing to the increased degradation of life on our planet.

So ethical tourism is defined *against* mass tourism, the latter caricatured as unethical and irresponsible. However, in this advocacy of ethical tourism, mass tourism is more than a reference to numbers of tourists – it is also, and more crucially, about a *type* of tourist. The use of the term 'mass' tends to carry pejorative connotations – unthinking, unaware and someone who simply follows the crowds. My dictionary definition is apposite: *mass*: 'an aggregate in which individuality is lost.' In this respect mass tourism is up there with supermarkets and cheap food as an exemplar of terrible mass consumption in modern, industrial, mass society, deemed destructive by ethical campaigners.

Ethical tourism advocate and tourism planning consultant Ahluwalia Poon sums up the state of the debate:

> The tourism industry is in crisis ... a crisis of mass tourism that has brought social, cultural, economic and environmental havoc in its wake, and it is mass tourism practices that must be radically changed to bring in the new.
>
> *Tourism, Technology and Competitive Strategy*, 1993

Backed up by such exaggerated claims, ethical tourism has effortlessly acquired the moral high ground *vis-à-vis* its mass package counterpart. In this vein, one European Union funded sustainable tourism project in Tenerife pledges support to 'Traditional communities under threat', the guilty party being mass tourism development which has pushed, 'An age old culture to the edge of extinction' (Proyecto Ambiental promotional literature, 1997). Such assertions target a caricature of package holidays and holiday resorts to present an essentially conservative, preservationist outlook – an outlook that is central to ethical tourism. Supporters of the project assist in compost making and help research the myths of the goat herders whilst casting a condemnatory (but perhaps occasionally envious) eye down to the brimming resorts beneath them on the coast, and beneath them morally.

Ethical tourism is a nasty crusade against a particular characterization of mass tourism and the mass tourist. Take, for example, the 'Three Ts' companies (travelling, trekking and trucking) which have gone out of their way to distance themselves from those offering the Three Ss (sun, sea and sand). One such, the travel company Explore, advertises its holidays as being 'For people who want more out of their holiday than buckets of cheap wine and a suntan.' The Community Tourist Guide is quick to differentiate its holidays from 'The bland façade of mainstream tourism' and the 'Tired tourist treadmill.' Some ethical campaigners clearly see the masses on holiday as a homogenous, unthinking crowd, lacking individuality. Those of us who dare to enjoy our holidays rather than seeing them as part of a personal moral mission are looked down upon as too cheap and cheerful, crude and unsophisticated.

ANTI-FUN AND ANTI-PEOPLE

Having fun and forgetting one's cares was what I thought holidays were all about. Not so, according to advocates of ethical tourism. Fun is viewed as a fraught affair. According to Alison Standcliffe of UK ethical tourism campaigners Tourism Concern, leaving your cares behind can mean 'Closing your eyes to the things you normally care about' (*Preserve or Destroy? Tourism and the Environment*, 1995, p.56). Green campaigner George Monbiot sums up the dim view taken of mainstream tourism when he asserts, 'Tourism is, by and large, an unethical activity, which allows us to have fun at everyone else's expense' (*Guardian*, 15 May 1999). Such a glum, killjoy outlook is not untypical of today's ethical tourism advocacy. Another author cites the 'Increasingly hedonistic philosophy of many people' as mitigating against ethical, sustainable tourism. Holidays were once associated with innocence and fun. Today, ethical tourism would have us guilt tripped.

Anthropologist Rupert Sheldrake, a character featured in David Lodge's novel *Paradise News*, typifies the spoilsport outlook of ethical advocates. Sheldrake travels to Hawaii and comments that, 'I am doing to tourism what Marx did to capitalism, what Freud did to family life. Deconstructing it.' Sheldrake travels alone – his perceptive fiancée ended their engagement; 'She said I spoiled her holidays, analysing them all the time.' Ethical tourism encourages us all to deconstruct our experiences, to dwell on our actions, to self-consciously audit our cultural and environmental impact – and to pass judgement on others who don't.

Advocates of ethical tourism, however, deny that ethical tourism is an albatross around the neck of fun seekers. Rather, they see it as an 'add on' that improves the whole experience. For example, *Being There*, a recently launched ethical tourism magazine, is marketed at 'Funky, adventurous, interesting and interested women who want to put something back into the local communities and destinations they visit on holiday.' Anita Roddick, pioneer of ethical consumption and co-founder of the magazine, adds that the places you visit 'Literally go(es) from being a holiday destination to a place where you can share, learn and grow' (Tourism Concern Press Release, 2001).

The implicit message here is that there is a great world of opportunity that naïve package tourists are missing out on. But why not let people decide on what they want from a holiday, free from moralizing about what constitutes worthy, ethical travel? Ethical brands are presented as more enjoyable and more fulfilling for tourists – but why not leave tourists to be the judge of what makes a good holiday for them? What ever happened to the customer is always right?

Far from being fulfilling, people-oriented holidays, ethical brands such as ecotourism can reflect a distinct disillusionment with 'people' – after all, isn't it about eschewing frivolity, crowds, cities and one's own society in search of a natural high? Ecotourism, along with other types of tourism that focus on experiencing a less modern existence – and most ethical tourism is of this ilk – is more likely to be introspective and egocentric. Such tourism often subscribes to the romantic notion that the self is to be found not in one's own society but in the solitary contemplation of cultures deemed to be closer to nature. The pristine environments and diverse cultures that ethical tourists hold dear are in fact simply the backdrop for the working out of their own post-modern, and distinctly anti-modern, angst. The mass tourist, on the other hand, enjoys conviviality, crowds and, of course, people. So which of the two types of tourism can really lay claim to being 'people centred'?

It is notable that the concern over ethical behaviour on holiday is no longer restricted to 'lager louts' of the Club 18–30 variety or even to consumers of the package holiday. In fact, the irony of ethical tourism is that the debate has moved full circle. Whilst originally, environmentally conscious tourists, tour operators and Non-Governmental Organizations criticized what they perceived to be the ravages of the mass tourism industry, and proposed 'new' forms of tourism such as ecotourism, alternative tourism, green tourism and community tourism as more progressive options, some of these proposed solutions now find themselves under scrutiny. The argument of the past was that mass tourism created concrete eyesores that paid no regard to the local environment and to traditional cultures. But more recently, 'ethical' alternatives such as ecotourism have themselves been criticized as a Trojan horse for the tourism industry – where the ecotourist treads, the less adventurous tourist may follow. Would it not, cynics argue, be better for tourists to stay in places in which they can be 'managed', and 'kept together in one place', thus liberating the wilderness from the threat of the tourist footprint? Are not, then, Blackpool and Benidorm the ultimate in sustainable, ethical tourism?

There is a logic in such arguments. But it is a logic premised on a profound cynicism that views tourists as problems to be controlled. In this view tourists become willing prisoners, sheep-like, residing in beachside jails.

NO MORE ADVENTURES

Ethical tourism turns out to be less a definitive list of what is ethical and what is unethical (although certain types of holiday are generally regarded as good and bad respectively). Instead, it is more of a fluid, moralistic perspective that resides on the notions of a surfeit of freedom for the tourist, and environmental and cultural fragility at the destination. Given this, it is unsurprising that backpackers, or 'mass backpackers' as they have been dubbed, are in the frame too.

Indeed, to be young and to travel these days seems to invite cynicism, if not downright hostility, from the ethical travel lobby. Libby Purves, writing in *The Times* in 2001, implores young travellers not to 'Travel light on morals', before going on to describe foreign backpackers in London as 'Great lumbering dung beetles ... slumping like so many uncollected bin bags around the Trafalgar Square fountain.' Whilst backpackers enjoy a rare freedom, it is a freedom which in the words of one critic, 'Threatens to engulf us', as ever more places and cultures become 'destinations' for the footloose traveller. Ethical tourism advocates the reigning in of this freedom through a critical self-awareness of one's potential complicity in trashing the planet and levelling cultures. One travellers' code of ethics puts it like this

> Away from home and free; it is tempting to do things I would never do. I shall avoid this danger by observing myself critically whilst on holiday and behave with restraint. I want to enjoy myself without hurting and offending others.
>
> Tourism With Insight 'Code of Conduct'

Codes of conduct for travellers and tourists abound, containing a range of advice including the following: 'Don't give money or sweets to children' (Tourism Concern); 'Be patient, friendly and sensitive. Remember, you are a guest' (Tourism Concern); 'Tourism is the world's largest industry. It can play an important role in maintaining indigenous cultures and is an invaluable source of foreign currency for many African countries. With a little consideration you can help to preserve this unique part of the world for future generations', (Friends of Conservation); 'Respect the frailty of the Earth. Realize that unless all are willing to help in its preservation, unique and beautiful destinations may not be here for future generations to enjoy' (Ten Commandments of Ecotourism – the American Society of Travel Agents).

The growth of such codes is a notable development especially in a pursuit traditionally associated with independence of mind and experimentation. Today, backpackers are subject to a plethora of preachy advice on how they should behave, where they should and should not go, and where they should spend their money. For many young backpackers, seeking to strike out and have an adventure, ethical tourism plays the role of 'the parent in your head', reminding you to clear up after yourself, be polite and to stay on the footpath.

The growth of codes of ethical conduct (now to be found in the *Rough Guides*, in-flight videos, and at your local travel agent) is exemplary of an important trend – that the negotiation of new countries and new cultures is increasingly presented as fraught with difficulty. Tourists must be on their guard at all times in case they should cause offence. They should interact with local cultures but at the same time maintain a respectful distance from these same cultures. Even whether or not to give money to beggars has come within the realm of the codes. This turning of basic human functions into ethical problems is at times striking – it is easy to forget that we are talking about something as prosaic as holidays.

The ethical code-makers treat young travellers like children, unable to think and act for themselves. This assumption threatens to demean the positive function of travel, as it shields people from confronting and dealing with problems for themselves. It eschews the taking of cultural risks and hence diminishes the possibilities of learning from our own mistakes. It limits free thinking by contributing to a climate of restraint. In effect the ethical codes tell us what the answer should be before we have even been confronted with the question. Whilst travel takes us to other places and other cultures, ethical tourism tries to ensure that our own risk averse and wary culture accompanies us, lest we should forget about it, let go, and start to have a real adventure.

A very different view of travel is that of Joseph Conrad, who described the origins of his thirst for travel thus, in his 1902 work *The Heart of Darkness*:

> Now when I was a little chap I had a passion for maps. I would look for hours at South America, or Africa or Australia, and lose myself in the glories of exploration. At that time there were

> many blank spaces on the Earth, and when I saw one that looked particularly inviting on a map (but they all look like that) I would put my finger on it and say, 'When I grow up I will go there.'

The spirit of this passage has inspired many, and although there are few, if any, 'blank spaces' on the Earth, the desire to travel simply through a sense of adventure and intrigue is strong. However, the ethical baggage associated with travel now threatens to shackle a spirit of adventure for travellers young and old. Today's travellers are increasingly counselled to be wary and cautious of their impact on people and places and to 'give something back'. But if travel is to really be a life-expanding activity or a unique experience, then it has to rely on and trust the individual, be they reckless or sensitive, impulsive or well prepared. Attempts to formalize codes of ethics can only contribute to a spirit of caution rather than one of adventure and discovery.

In fact, the attempt to provide guidelines for individual conduct on holiday is misguided. The advice offered is often derived from a *particular* ethical outlook, one that stresses the pre-eminence of nature over development, but that is then presented as a universal set of rules for all. Tourists to the developing world may seek to spend their holiday cash in a local community rather than in hotels. This may yield some limited benefits for the rural community, but cut into the service economy in the towns and cities. Refuse to buy a coral necklace and you may contribute to coral preservation, but the vendor may be a little poorer as a result. If we campaign against golf courses on the basis of their use of water supplies, we may conserve the latter but deny people the income from high spending golf tourists and the consequent possibilities for improving infrastructure. There can therefore be no rules or codes that apply generally. These codes are more about regulating tourists than helping the country of destination. Individuals may decide differently in different circumstances for a variety of reasons – these are matters for consideration and debate. To try to regulate these decisions by drawing up ethical guidelines is a foolish task. It suggests surrogate parenthood – something young travellers perhaps felt they were leaving at home. Even more foolish is to take conservation as the starting point, when in the developing world societies to which the codes are most frequently applied, *development*, not imposed ideas of conservation, is such a pressing need.

CREATING MISUNDERSTANDING

Whilst highly circumspect about people's freedom to holiday as they wish, ethical tourism advocates do invoke a type of freedom – freedom *from* tourists (or at least the wrong type of tourist). Societies, particularly rural societies, are viewed as being under threat from tourism and self-appointed spokespeople for these societies seek to defend what they see as the authenticity and integrity of traditional communities.

In this vein the Proyecto Ambiental Tenerife sustainable tourism project asserts its aim as being: 'To help sustain the rich diversity of human life on earth.' It seeks to achieve this aim by encouraging volunteers to take conservation holidays during which participants can assist with traditional farming techniques and the marketing of craft products. It is held that outside influences, such as the mass tourism on the island, threaten to create, 'A monotonous sea of uniformity.' Ethical initiatives see their role as maintaining rural cultures in the face of this cultural assault. The mission statement puts it bluntly: 'Respect for the local culture … this must be absolute.'

Underpinning this reverence for the culture of the host community is the view that people, host and tourist, are defined by their differences. It is a view that is central to ethical tourism advocacy. Cultural *difference* is assumed as a starting point whilst *common* aspirations and desires shared by host and tourist are rarely considered. Arising from this there is an emphasis on, and guarded approach to, cultural contact. There is a tendency to treat contact between tourists and their hosts as a constant cultural dilemma, in the manner of David Lodge's anthropologist, Rupert Sheldrake. The growth of ethical codes exemplifies the view that tourist and host are *so* different that we simply cannot get on together without a set of ethical rules to guide us.

The truth, however, is more straightforward. An acquaintance of mine recounted to me his experience of a holiday in St Lucia. He asked a waitress earnestly about her way of life because this, of course, is the sort of thing a thinking ethical tourist should do. The waitress wore traditional dress, in keeping with the expectations of the customers, and recited a hammed-up account of the rural way of life further inland. In the context of such role playing it is difficult to discover empathy or commonality. My acquaintance was studying at University. The young woman was saving hard in order to travel and, hopefully, study abroad. Only after a few drinks and a loosening of cultural mores did they uncover their common aspirations. Material inequality divided them, not a fetishised 'culture'. The thrill of travel is that barriers can be stripped away and real friendships made. Ethical tourism stresses cultural differences and the need to 'respect' them and be 'sensitive' tourists. But an over-sensitivity to supposed cultural difference can easily blind us to a common humanity, diminishing the potential to learn from each other and enjoy each other's company.

Viewing the host and tourist in terms of *cultures* is characteristic of the ethical critique of tourism. Ethical tourism presents host and tourist as inhabiting two separate worlds, with a cultural divide in between. In this vein, anthropologists have turned their hand to the study of tourism, regarding it as a form of acculturation, meaning 'Culture change that is initiated by the conjunction of *two or more cultural systems*' (D. Nash, *The Anthropology of Tourism*, 1996, my emphasis). Clearly, if we begin with different 'cultural systems' then what hosts and tourists have in common may be overlooked. The emphasis on the tourists' culture posing a threat to that of the host generates sympathy, but creates a barrier to empathy.

For example, volunteers on the Earthwatch Amazonian Cultural Tradition holiday record the rich oral traditions of the people of Pirabas, traditions that are 'threatened by the cannonade of modern culture, namely television' (Earthwatch publicity leaflet). Here the desire to protect the host's culture from our own seems to extend to a desire to deny them a television set. It is often the ethical tourist who decides what is and what is not appropriate for the host population. The consequence of morally elevating the defined culture of one's host in this fashion is evident in Sir Crispin Tickell's remark, referring to tourism in less economically developed regions, that humanity should, 'Glory in our differences rather than subordinate ourselves to some grey middle standard.' (Foreword to *Ecotourism: A Sustainable Option*, 1994.) Such assertions begin a commitment to equality – it seems that the ethical tourist would rather host countries are preserved to their liking, regardless of poverty.

Taking a similar tack in the BBC's *Our Man In Goa*, Clive Anderson exclaims that '[Tourists should] find somewhere else to go, with a culture that is not so fragile and with very little of value that can actually be damaged ... somewhere like Eurodisney' (BBC TV,

1995). Not only is Goa's culture deemed fundamentally different, but it is both more fragile and more valuable than the tourist's own. This deference to a romanticized sense of the host's culture can only erect new barriers between peoples. In reality, many of Goa's inhabitants are positive about tourism, not least because of the economic benefits it brings. Aspirations for material gain and more equality are often overlooked in ethical advocacy. In gazing at culture, it is easy to miss *people* – people with similar aspirations to ourselves.

The assumption of the *primacy* of cultural difference has become an unhelpful dogma within much of the advocacy of ethical tourism. The formal counter position of *cultures*, that of the host and that of the tourist, means that ethical advocates rarely approach their subject from the perspective of *commonality*. That the host and tourist may share common needs, desires and aspirations is not considered. Not least of these may be the aspiration to join the growing but very limited ranks of the world's tourists, an aspiration only achievable in the context of economic growth and cultural change. It seems that somewhere in the promotion of cultural sensitivity, the aspiration for understanding and equality has been lost.

Tourism involves contact between peoples from different regions and cultures. While some see risks in terms of cultural imperialism, it can also be the case that preconceived notions of difference are broken down. It is not unusual to experience culture shock in reverse – we expect a world of difference but discover people who aspire to the same things as we do, who think about similar questions and issues, be it within quite different situations. Part of the thrill of travel is to meet and connect with people outside of one's own community or culture. But to view the host as a cultural icon, representative of a society unsullied by modern life, is to diminish the potential in the tourist experience for both host and tourist. Over sensitivity to otherness blinds us to common humanity.

CONCLUSION – BETTER OFF AT HOME?

The logic of the angst ridden ethical critique is that tourism should be *for* something – something more, that is, than enjoyment and relaxation. In this vein, one advocate of ecotourism demands: 'Tourism remains a passive luxury for thousands of travellers. This must change'.

In place of luxury, the ethical tourism creed is that tourism has to be part of a particular moral agenda that places culture on a pedestal and cites the humble tourist as a major threat. Some forms of tourism, those that are deemed respectful (by ethical tourists) of other people and places, are OK, whilst simple pleasure seeking is implicitly condemned as damaging. In this vein, well-travelled green advocate George Monbiot argues that travel is beneficial for '...the few for whom travel does broaden the mind' and goes on to say that 'Whilst they number as tens among the millions, their enlightenment surely means that tourism, for all its monstrosities, cannot be condemned' (*The Green Travel Guide*, 1998). For the holier than thou critics of our holidays, tourism is justified only when it is part of a moral agenda pertaining to their particular view of the value of diverse cultures. In the name of ethical tourism, this is presented to us as a universal standard for all concerned people to follow.

If we do not subscribe to this agenda, we are unethical tourists, and by George Monbiot's reckoning, excrescences upon the natural world – we'd be better off staying at home! Indeed, this is precisely the conclusion drawn by Jenny Jones of the Green Party who was moved by the Newbury bypass to assert the following:

> How many residents of Newbury have been there: if more of them realised what they are about to lose local opposition to the bypass would be insurmountable. Will they instead allow the road to be built, and eventually use it to drive to Europe, to spend a holiday somewhere in the countryside not unlike what is being trashed on their doorstep?
>
> 'Can Tourism Be Green?', *Green World*, March 1996

Not only do such pronouncements paint a picture of a naïve or uncaring tourist, but there is a certain hypocrisy in calls for restraint such as these. Jones, without a hint of irony, lists at the end of her article that she has worked and travelled in Jordan, Syria, Israel, Turkey, Crete, Ethiopia, Cyprus, Egypt and Abu Dhabi, as well as having lived in the Seychelles and Lesotho. A case of do as I say, not as I do?

Tourism is being recast as an arena for moral proscription and critical self-awareness. It is no longer good enough to travel footloose and fancy free. Tourism is accompanied by constant warnings to limit one's behaviour and to be ethical. From the environmental group Arc's pamphlet 'Sun, Sea Sand and Saving the World' to Friends of the Earth's advice to question whether you *need* to travel at all, tourism is now the terrain of ethical codes and not a little guilt tripping. The often impulsive and reckless desire to strike out across Europe or further afield is no longer a good enough reason. The traveller seeking adventure is circumscribed. The sun worshipper is frowned upon. The fun lover is reminded that they are complicit in a 'destructive industry'. In the name of ethical tourism, leisure travel has never been subject to such moral proscription, that we would enjoy our holidays more and get to know each other better without it.

Essay Five

ENFORCED PRIMITIVISM

Kirk Leech

The United Nations has designated 2002 as the International Year of Ecotourism. In co-ordination with the United Nations Commission on Sustainable Development, it has mandated the United Nations Environment Programme (UNEP) and the World Tourism Organization to carry out international activities promoting ecotourism. Ecotourism, it is argued, is socially responsible, enlightened travel, that stresses the need to be wary of man's impact on the environment and respects the cultures of indigenous communities. Advocates of ecotourism see it as the means to resolve the conflicting demands of conservation and development and to help satisfy the growing demand for wilderness and sanctuary areas where development is regulated. One of the key aesthetic aspects of the ecotourist experience is the opportunity to travel to human-free wildlife areas such as parks and sanctuaries. It gives us, we are told, the opportunity to experience the genuine, the authentic and the sensitive without damaging the environment and 'corrupting' the lives of indigenous people. It is seen as the 'real', 'natural' and 'sustainable experience' for today's international traveller.

The conservation aspect of ecotourism has led to it being endorsed by international environmental Non-Governmental Organizations (NGOs) such as the World Conservation Union and the World Wildlife Fund (WWF). Supporters of these NGOs argue that the planet needs sanctuaries and wilderness areas because of the ecologically destructive impact of man. Their argument is that ecosystems are the innocent victim of human malfeasance, and the answer is the exclusion or regulation of human activity from large areas of the planet. Consequently they are strong advocates of low-impact ecotourism activities that are ecologically benign and economically profitable.

For those concerned with development, ecotourism does seem on the surface to be a means to benefit local communities. The World Bank believes ecotourism to be a niche market with significant advantages – visitors spend more money and stay longer, leading to greater income generation for local people. The British Department for International Development promotes schemes that advocate what it calls 'pro-poor tourism' and USAID, financed by the US Government, does the same. They see ecotourism as being more than just a useful revenue source for countries: it plays a major role in developing those nations' economies and infrastructures. This is seen as 'pro-poor tourism' providing a variety of revenue opportunities. Ecotourism depends on areas of natural beauty to attract visitors and revenue. As 'pristine beauty' is what travellers want, and are willing to pay vast sums to visit, revenue can be used for their up-keep and for benefit to local people. It is claimed that those living in these areas will be the main beneficiaries of safeguarding the environment and, as 'stakeholders', play a key role in their up-keep.

Visitor numbers to such projects are notoriously inaccurate. No major study has been carried out which determines what part of tourism is based on ecotourist 'principles'. But what is certain is that studies show that 50 per cent of nature tourists seek to include a visit to a natural park or wilderness area during their visit. Travel by individuals or small groups to relatively untouched natural areas, where they can experience the natural environment and encounter local people directly, has been increasing rapidly in the last two decades, indicating shifts away from the more popular destinations of northern and southern Europe towards nature-based destinations. The growth in the number of protected areas is certainly indisputable. Over 300 million hectares of the world are now described by the World Conservation Union as wilderness, there are over 5,000 protected areas worldwide including wilderness areas, parks and sanctuaries. With financial backing from the World Bank and others more land is being designated to be wilderness and sanctuary.

In this essay, I will argue that this outcome of the determination to protect vast areas of land for conservation projects is in fact far from beneficial for the people whose countries have become the primary destinations for the ecotourist. The impulse to conserve, and that of ecotourism, is informed both by a deep-seated cynicism about man's relationship to nature, and by nineteenth-century colonialist ideas of elite areas to be enjoyed by the enlightened amongst us. Ecotourism activities are of no long-term benefit to local communities. Local people face expulsion from their land, increased regulation of their lives, and a future based on small-scale nature centred development schemes – all to satisfy both a conservation dream and a romantic western search for spiritual well-being.

SANCTUARY, SANCTUARY

Sanctuaries are places we crave to escape to, to hide in, and to repair ourselves. They are a perfect twenty-first century response to a life that seems to go too fast. The world's wildernesses are seen as sanctuaries, allowing privileged western visitors to experience wild untamed nature.

Ecotourist company travel brochures often denigrate 'normal' holidays, 'You didn't feel changed by the experience: you came back the same person you were before you left' whilst extolling the life-changing ecotourism experience. 'Imagine visiting an un-crowded, actively preserved coastline or rainforest, guided by locals who are ready and able to explain the natural wonders before you.' 'Take part in a ceremonial dance on the beach under the stars. Local guides are ready and willing to translate and interpret', with the added opportunity to 'meet with local people in their homes.' We can 'Live the true Borneo experience', or alternatively we can trek 'over ancient stones once trod by the Incas, traversing mountain passes, and pausing by ancient ceremonial centers that still ring with the spirit of those turbulent times.' But, alternatively, maybe the 'Rainforest adventure is for you if you are looking for a tropical unspoiled jungle environment and want to experience nature in its purist form on this 4-day package.'

Though many of us crave sanctuaries away from the modern world, the idea of wilderness areas where tourists can sample nature, free of man, is a western romantic illusion. And further, what is evident is that the preservation of these areas comes at a very high cost to local communities which are either removed from the land, have their lives regulated or are forced to play the role of theme park extras to satisfy the demands of ecotourism.

The fight to keep man out of wilderness areas is a long one. In late-nineteenth century America, a movement and mood developed that saw wildernesses as a sanctuary from the modern world – human-free areas that should be vacated for the rehabilitation and resurrection of the human spirit. Led by American Romantics such as John Muir, Aldo Leopold and Ralph Waldo Emerson, this form of Romanticism was part of the reaction to the onset of industrialization. They fought to keep wilderness areas such as Yosemite, Sequoia and the Grand Canyon human-free, creating in 1872 the world's first protected area – Yellowstone Park. In the process, the resident population of Shoshone Indians was expelled, and as many as 300 are believed to have been killed by the US Cavalry. Muir and his followers saw the conservation and preservation of nature as being beneficial for human spiritual and physical well-being, the Shoshone were clearly thought to be beyond such concerns.

This exclusion outlook became the viewpoint of the developing national parks programme in the USA and subsequently that of global conservation. Ideas of wilderness and the exclusion of the local community coalesced very easily with nineteenth-century colonialist ideas, particularly in Britain. Muir's template became effectively the global conservation position.

THE REAL IMPACT ON LOCAL COMMUNITIES OF WILDERNESS PRESERVATION

There are now some 5,000 protected areas that cover three per cent of the land on Earth. The vast majority of these parks, wildlife preserves and sanctuaries are created on already populated land. In Latin America, it is estimated that 86 per cent of protected areas were already populated. In India, over three million people live inside the country's 500 national parks and sanctuaries. The history of many of today's protected areas has been one of exclusion and expulsion of the local community and of increasing regulation of their use. The conservationist Bernard Grzimek, whose work in East Africa turned the Serengeti Plains into the most famous protected areas in the world, argued forcefully in the 1960s for the native Masai to be excluded from their land. Grzimek believed that a national park should remain a primordial wilderness to be effective and that no men, not even native ones, should live inside its borders. The Masai, nomadic inhabitants of the Ngorongoro crater in Tanzania, were pressured and offered inducements to leave the crater, to allow a wildlife sanctuary to be developed. Their subsequent inability to seek out a decent standard of living for themselves led to widespread criticism of moves that had left them on the margins.

One of the consequences of creating a standard model of park creation is that it makes the removal of people from national parks often the norm, resettlement being part of the legal requirement for park creation, even though it may be evident that the continued presence of these people threatens nothing but western conservationist sensibilities, and is certainly not a bio-diversity threat.

Cameroon has over one one-fifth of its land devoted to parks and reserves, many used for ecotourism. The creation of the Korup National Park, a 126,000 hectare forest where over 1,000 people lived, was praised by the WWF as a model plan integrating economic development and conservation. The establishment of the park meant resettling the local community, moves which were supported by the WWF. This led to a huge row, as surveys showed that people being resettled were unlikely to threaten the declared aims of the park. As one herdsman stated in Fred Pearce's 1999 book *The Green Warriors* (published by Bodley Head):

> These parks were created for white men, who can still hunt in the parks, and do what ever they want. We didn't even know the park existed until the authorities started sending our people to prison for hunting. That was when we found out we were not allowed to hunt the wild animals that were killing our livestock. Why didn't anyone ask us what we thought?

When the local community is allowed to remain, their lives are heavily regulated. The WWF has been involved in setting up nature reserves around the edge of the Sahara desert. Its flagship project was the Air and Tenere National Nature Reserve in the Air Massif, close to the desert area of Niger. The WWF and the Niger Government decided to let the region's 3,000 nomadic people, largely Tuareg herders, carry on living in a reserve twice the size of Switzerland, but only on the understanding that activities such as hunting and protecting cattle would be controlled. In the project, 'development' was the pay-off for the loss of 10,000 square kilometres that became a 'strict nature reserve'. Within the reserve, all hunting was banned, as was protecting animals from predators such as jackals, a real cost for people whose main occupation is cattle herding. As for development, the major plan was to introduce tourism into the area. It was recognized at the time by one WWF representative that the Tuareg would see little of the money.

In 1994, the WWF used the slogan: 'He's destroying his own rainforest. To stop him, do you send in the army or an anthropologist [to raise funds]?' Critic of environmentalism Ton Dietz suggests that this was an 'ecototalitarian approach' and those local communities which do not behave in accordance with the new environmental norms are criminalized and penalized (*Entitlement to Natural Resources*, International Books, 1996).

It was programmes such as the one in Cameroon that led some to reconsider Muir's preservation and exclusion ethic. Evidence was stacking up that local communities were increasingly being penalized as the environment was privileged over human interests. Within development circles, this led to attempts to find a way to reconcile the development needs of local people or conservation. I now turn to consider this project and its outcomes.

THE PROBLEM OF ECOTOURISM

The language of ecotourism and community tourism is that of local stakeholders, empowerment, development and community involvement, rather than simply conservation and preservation of the land. It thus appears to be an approach that is conscious of the need to avoid riding roughshod over the interests of local people. Much evidence suggests that the notion that there is a genuine collaboration between local people and NGOs is far from accurate.

Krishna Ghimire, project leader at the United Nations Research Institute for Social Development, argues, for example, that the well-documented examples of local participation in such schemes were 'designed principally to reduce conflicts over parks rather than to offer sustainable livelihood alternatives to local people' ('Parks and people', in *Development and Change*, **25**, 1, January 1994). Ole Kamuaro comments that 'Rarely have local people been involved in planning and implementation of ecotourism ventures' (*Eco-tourism: Suicide or Development?*, United Nations Non-Governmental Liason Service, 1996). Ecotourism, for these critics, represents both an idealized version of what wilderness areas are, and of the people who live in them. For Kamuaro, the aim of ecotourism ventures are to stimulate the tourist's nostalgic desire for the authentic and the untouched, providing that local people are ready and available for discovery by tourists. The possibility that indigenous people might not share the environmental concerns of ecotourism's advocates, or wish to be actors in the new conservation theme parks, rarely enters the debate.

Advocates of ecotourism who recognize hostility at the local level believe the answer lies in community education. But it is increasingly clear that many local communities do not share Western conservationists' perceptions of wilderness and wildlife conservation and are unwilling to be actors in an ecotourist Disneyland. Nlaka'pamux local Ruby Dustan echoed such views about the Stein Valley in Alberta, Canada – land she has lived on for decades. 'I never thought of the Stein Valley as wilderness,' she said. 'My dad used to say "that's our pantry"...some of the white environmentalists seemed to think if something was declared a wilderness, no one was allowed inside because it was fragile, the romantic notions in people's heads are food in our heads' (quoted in M. Colchester, 'Salvaging Nature: Indigenous Peoples and Protected Areas' in K. B. Ghimire and M. P. Pimbert (eds), *Social Change and Conservation: Environmental Politics and the Impacts of National Parks and Protected Areas*, Earthscan, 1997). Other research by scholar Elizabeth Kempf found a similar disparity between locals' views and those of conservationists. One of her interviewees, a cattle herdsmen in the Fari National Park in Cameroon, explained 'These parks were created for white men who can still hunt in the parks and do what ever they want. We didn't know the parks existed until the authorities started sending our people to prison for hunting (*Indigenous People and Protected Areas*, Sieera Books, 1994).

The WWF itself has found that its own claims regarding 'empowerment' and 'local participation' are overblown. After 25 years of campaigning and promoting national parks in Africa, WWF carried out a survey to discover what local communities thought of their work. Sally Zalewski of WWF France spent two years questioning rural people in West Africa. The findings of her studies were a shock to WWF and never published. The survey showed that local people were unaware of the existence of many national parks. The highest 'don't know' count, 74 per cent, came from people living close to the Nikola Koba National Park in eastern Senegal.

These findings were doubly embarrassing to WWF, as one of its mobile education units had been based near the park at Tambacounda for a number of years. Even the panda symbol of the WWF, widely known in the developed world, means little to local villagers. Zalewski recounts that most villagers were curious about the animal, asking where it lived, whether it existed in their county, and whether it could be eaten.

However, when the local community decides that it does not want to live as visiting ecotourists expect, it may face hostility. As Robert Gordon found in his research when a group of San (Bushmen) living in the Kalahari Gemsbok National Park in South Africa requested some of the meager comforts of the modern world – better housing and new clothes – park wardens reacted with anger 'as their desirability as a tourist attraction was under serious doubt' (quoted in M. Colchester, 'Salvaging Nature: Indigenous Peoples and Protected Areas' op.cit.). At the very least, they are expected to perform. Journalist Sue Armstrong, investigating the same park, pointed out that when some ecotourists saw people wearing normal clothes, 'their first question is always where are the Bushmen?' ('A landless people of the land', *Electronic Mail & Guardian*, 11 July, 1996).

Survival International itself has found that where they do 'perform', other Bushmen are certainly not doing what they would if it were not for ecotourism. They are playing the preconceived role required by tourists. 'The scene is a Bushman's camp in remote Botswana. In the distance a plume of dust shows the arrival of a (tourist) jeep. The people, what ever they are doing, quickly pull off their T-shirts, trousers and cotton dresses, and begin to dance' (Mowforth and Munt, *Tourism and Sustainability: New Tourism in the Third World*, Routledge, 1998). Using the Bushmen as a tourist attraction has been called 'zooification' by the academics Mowforth and Munt.

Local people in fact often appear clear about the advantages of ecotourism (and the consequent demand on them to act 'authentic') – it brings them money. But they are equally clear that they are hostile to its costs. Masai of Kenya, who opposed moves by the director of the Kenya Wildlife Services to make them less dependent on herding cattle but more dependent on tourism, suggested to journalist George Monbiot in 1999, 'We know there is money to be made from tourism. We already have tourists staying on our lands in tented camps. And yes, they bring us an income. We don't need the Kenya Wildlife Service to tell us that. But you can tell Dr Leaky this: We don't want to be dependent on these tourists. We are Masai and we want to heard cattle' (George Monbiot, 'Whose wildlife is it anyway?', *Electronic Mail & Guardian*, 9 June 1999). In Africa, the creation of some of the world's most beautiful parks and reserves has also been found to come at a high cost for local communities. Dhynai Berger, a Kenyan wildlife consultant, has commented that in order to survive the Masai have been reduced to trinket sellers. Journalist Sue Armstrong describes a preserve where Bushmen, who are themselves the main tourist attraction, are allowed to hunt but only with bows and arrows: 'Lions regularly take their donkeys and goats at night... but Bushman may not hunt the animals' ('A landless people of the land', *Electronic Mail & Guardian*, 11 July 1996).

In the Kagga Kamma Game Park north of Cape Town, tourists can pay to see an ad hoc group of Bushmen perform traditional rituals. With little economic opportunity outside of tourism, the Bushmen dress in skins and their prepubescent children dance for money. However, one game lodge owner rejected the group, suggesting that they did not look like the genuine article! (Eddie Koch, 'Whose land is this?', *Electronic Mail & Guardian*, 23 February 1995). For some, the authenticity of the Bushmen was not a problem. The general manager for a planned ecotourist project in Mozambique sought to import some of the Kalahari Bushmen into Mozambique, and told the journalist Eddie Koch that,

> If I get my way, I'll bring some of those little guys out here. Can you imagine tourists on the steam train looking out of one of the windows and seeing elephants and rhino? Then they'll look out of the other and see the little bastards running around with their loin clothes and poison tipped arrows. The way I see it we'll bring them rhino here and save them from going extinct so why not bring the little guys who are also going extinct
>
> Eddie Koch, 'The Texan who plans a dream park just here', *Electronic Mail & Guardian*, 18 January 1996

Some people have been even less fortunate. Female Burmese refugees from the Karenni tribe now living in Thailand, 'famous for their long necks', are being held in virtual slavery, 'as a tourist attraction in a human zoo' ('Amazing Thailand', *BBC World Service online*, 21 March 1999). Visits to the long-necked woman are part of package tours for tourists, along with elephant rides and trips to old opium dens. There was a failed plan to relocate all the women to a model-village in the capital, Rangoon, where they would live out their lives as tourist attraction. The World Bank estimates that over three million people have been removed from their land between 1986 and 1996.

THIS IS NOT DEVELOPMENT

Advocates of ecotourism and community tourism from NGOs and governments see themselves as promoting development and defending indigenous people. In the language of cultural diversity, sustainability and appropriate technology, they argue that these small-scale programmes are best for the developing world. But this is a new definition of development for the developing world, in which small-scale tourism is considered as a means to overcome a lack of development. The lack of vision apparent in these projects is astounding and outrageous, given that many host countries lack basic infrastructure or substantial industry, and have been left with no option but to exploit their natural resources. Yet long-gone are the advocates of large-scale, fundamental economic change.

Ecotourism cements the local community into a relationship with nature that makes development and progress reliant on using the natural capital available rather than moving away from a reliance on nature or agriculture. It explicitly links the well-being of the local population with environmental concerns. The fact that one sees tourism as a revenue source for countries is one thing, and there is nothing intrinsically wrong in people enjoying these types of holidays and activities, but to see it as the means for substantial development reveals a degraded sense of what development is.

To have a transformative impact, development must change the relationship of man to the natural world. Ecotourist projects confirm man's subordination to nature. Such policies are not a palliative to the loss of even meager income from being displaced from your land or having your economic activities regulated. Small-scale development as compensation for removal from land is the uncomfortable reality. This approach effectively freezes people into a relationship with nature that confirms the idea that these societies will never be able to transform themselves beyond being stewards of the environment. As geographer and critic of ecotourism Jim Butcher has argued, 'Community tourism provides answers for conservationists confronted with the accusation that they are only concerned with the environment, but fewer to the question of development itself' (*The Moralisation of Tourism*, Routledge, 2002).

As the examples of The Hluhluwe-Umfolozi National Game Park in South Africa and of Belize (detailed below), illustrate, ecotourism programmes that claim to offer a new development approach are far from being an option that delivers a free and independent choice for the host countries. Relations between the developed and developing world are unfairly weighted in the political and economic spheres. The idea that developing world countries can withstand the economic weight of the developed world and the political pressure of international NGOs is laughable.

THE HLUHLUWE-UMFOLOZI NATIONAL GAME PARK, SOUTH AFRICA

Tourist brochures for The Hluhluwe-Umfolozi Park claim that the park is 'renowned for its variety of animal and bird life, its wide-ranging photography, and an extremely rich diversity of tree and plant communities', but as John Vidal's investigation of one of South Africa's most celebrated game parks shows, the consequences for the local community of its creation as an ecotourist destination have been disastrous ('A great white Lie', The *Guardian*, 1 December 2001).

The 25,000-hecatre savannah was the traditional hunting ground for colonialists and, before that, for Zulu kings. Today, western tourists can sleep in swanky hotels and bush lodges, tour the 'wilderness', and observe the charismatic animals – lions, leopards, elephants, rhino and giraffe – many people in the West so admire (from the safe distance of Land-Rovers).

The area is designated a wilderness, and development is outlawed. There are no roads or buildings, no telephone or electricity lines, no wells, wires, pumps, pipes, cultivation or development. No people may live here and no cars may enter by law. Entering this 'pristine' area you have to follow a strict formal etiquette. White guides instruct you not to leave any rubbish, you are asked to say a few words in the way of ritual, asking permission to enter the area. And as Vidal points out, to erase all trace of human impact, you are asked to 'bury your faeces'.

The land, though, is a cultural creation. It is a 'white lie'. Far from being a wild untamed land it is as controlled and artificial as the Eden Centre in Devon. Charismatic animals, as in many game parks, have been introduced from other areas and far from the animals being untouched some have been culled for money. Man has sculptured the land, grasses have been burnt back to encourage certain species to prosper, and the whole area has been fenced off preventing local people from returning.

It is clear what visitors to Umfolozi's wilderness are seeking. 'Wilderness is a sacred, archetypal place,' says Ian Player, brother of famous golfer Gary. 'These areas are modern temples. People should not live in the wilderness, but come and go' (J. Vidal, op cit). These are not just wildlife lovers, but people seeking a life-enhancing experience through a close encounter with nature, red in tooth and claw. The spiritual impact of wild places on human consciousness is the park's biggest selling point.

To achieve such a mythical idyll and preserve 'pure' African landscapes for western consumption could be accomplished only through separating the land from daily human activities, and settling them aside as national parks where humans enter only on holiday. Wildlife protection, like other imposed policies, has always carried with it the implications of force, of quasi-military operations, and of sanctions.

Environmental NGOs have been involved in militarized anti-poaching campaigns. In 1989, the WWF provided the Kenyan

Government with money to help crack down on ivory poachers. The money went towards operating five aircraft used in anti-poaching operations in the Tsavo National Park. Journalists later reported that the 'get tough' campaign against poachers involved spotter planes, 'helicopter gun ships', and local game wardens, 'molded into paramilitary fighting men with shoot to kill orders.' Over 30 poachers were killed; as one reporter said, 'it was more akin to the Green Berets than Green peace' (quoted in F. Pearce, *The Green Warriors*, Bodley Head, 1991).

BELIZE

In *The Making of Belize*: Globalization in the Margins (Bergin & Garvey, 1998), Anne Sutherland argues that Belize never developed a manufacturing based economy and became an ecotourist destination for those from industrial societies because of the absence of modernism. She suggests that tourism blossomed precisely because the country had not developed. Belize is now a country dominated by ecotourism, and far from benefiting the local population it is condemning them to a narrow form of economic development dependent on the fluctuating whims of foreign tourists.

Belize's reputation as one of the world's last wilderness areas developed during the 1980s. International environmental NGOs arrived in Belize as it gained independence in 1981. The newly established nation, with a limited economic base and virtually no development, was a rich and easy picking for the 'New Missionaries' of the environment. They lobbied and cajoled government, offered financial inducements and have been so successful in buying their way into government departments that they have taken responsibility for not only writing environmental laws but administering the running of parks and preserves. The financially and politically weak state in the country was unable to repel the seduction of environmentalists and ecotourist operators.

Within a remarkably short period of time, vast areas of Belize were turned into protected areas, and local people's access was restricted. By 1993 over 6,000 square kilometres had been converted, this is over one-third of the country. However, this is not enough for some – John Howell of the Natural History Museum of Belmopan wants to turn 50 per cent of the country's landmass into preserves. The result of all these developments is that a large portion of Belize consists of nature reserves positioned next to ecotourism areas, making Belize an ideal ecotourist destination and where tourism that does not meet the correct ecological standards is prevented.

The library of tour guidebooks such as *Lonely Planet*, *Rough Guide* and the *Sierra Club* magazine discovered Belize in the early 1990s. Its transformation from a secret destination for ethical and ecotourism to a most favoured destination has been rapid. Belize now receives more visitors every year than there are Belizeans living there. In 1993 the estimated number of visitors was 260,056 – 55,000 more than the number of people living there. According to estimates for 2000, the 'service' sector of the Belizean economy in which tourism represents the overwhelming part, made up 58 per cent of the country's Gross Domestic Product (*CIA World Factbook*, 2001). The importance of tourism to Belize is indicated by the fact that it is the only country in the world where the Minister for Tourism is also the Minister for the Environment, permanently cementing the link between tourism and the environment.

Belize has received plaudits for its creation as an ethical tourist paradise, being voted ecotourism destination in 1995, by *Caribbean and World* magazine. Travel companies, tourists and developers have helped create and recreate Belize in an image of their choosing. The establishment of parks, nature reserves and tourist resorts has shaped the Belizean land and economy, but what has been the impact of this development for Belizeans?

Some have benefited from the influx of foreign finance. Tourism is now second only to agriculture in importance to the Belizean economy. But the creation of Belize as an ecotourist destination could be accomplished only with the construction of vast areas of protected land where the local community was expelled and their activities controlled. Conservationist Alan Rabinowitz in *Jaguar; Struggle and Triumph in the Jungles of Belize* (Arbor House, 1986), in his account of his two-year stint in the world's first jaguar reserve, Cockscomb Jaguar Reserve in Belize, praises the support his efforts to save the Jaguars gained from the local Mayan people. However, in the arrogant style of many conservationists, he believes that the local Maya have to be removed from their land to safeguard the future of Jaguars through the creation of a nature reserve.

Many environmentalists welcomed the removal of Indian families and the shift towards ecotourism. Earthwatch Institute, one of the leading US environmentalist organizations, claimed that the project was an outstanding success where ecotourism replaced what had been 'destructive ways of making a living'. They went on to suggest that 'Despite initial resentment, the local population gradually began to see economic benefits from ecotourism after a local school teacher was hired as sanctuary director' (Earthwatch Institute, 'Two tickets to paradise. Is eco-tourism an environmental boon or boondoggle?', Nov/Dec, 1996). The removed Indians robbed of their land now wait outside the preserve hawking whatever they can invent as examples of authentic Belize to tourists visiting the land they have been removed from. If there are any substantial economic benefits from the project they have certainly not trickled down to the Maya.

Sutherland, a writer and a native of Belize, is horrified by what she calls the 'New Missionaries', Western environmental NGOs who have replaced Christian sects propagating their evangelical mission with their environmentalist zeal. They have now taken hold of 40 per cent of Belizean landmass, preserving it for ecotourists and ethical tourists to observe nature and visit archeological sites. Local communities in Belize, as in Africa, quickly discover that their traditional attempts at self-survival, their subsistence activities, are now criminalized.

In 1993 the UNDP, which is sponsoring 2002 as Ecotourist Year, admitted in a report that over 37 per cent of the population of Belize depended on the costal area for their living. Even so, it argued for the preservation of the costal area and the opportunity it provides for ecotourist adventures. Belize, as with wildlife parks in Africa, has seen the use of military means to prevent development and keep local people off their land. On 21 February 1997, the Belizean Defence Force surrounded a village close to the Guatemalan border and destroyed the crops of local people whom they accused of farming on reserve land.

The poetry of local man Adalbert Tucker sums up the plight of the people:

> In the name of the Jaguar,
> Please reserve some land for me.
> With the blessing of the butterfly
> Leave an acre for me
> The same is true of my friend the hiccatee:
> How come I am the problem
> only recently
> speaking environmentally
> and forgetting humanity

In the name of the Jaguar
And in the name of the Baboon
Leave an acre of sanctuary
for Belizean man and Belizean women
and another one for Belizean children.
We are like baboons with out a sanctuary
On the edge of marginality's marginality

In A. Sutherland, *The Making of Belize, Globalisation in the Margins*, 1998 (Bergin & Westport)

As Sutherland asks, 'for whom are all the reserves in Belize?'

CONCLUSION

Advocates of ecotourism see it as the means to overcome the conflicting demands and pressures of conservation and development. It allows limited access to areas of wilderness and sanctuary, while at the same time rewarding local communities for their involvement with holidays and their stewardship of the environment. Whilst seemingly an advance on previous ideas which sought just to exclude local people from their land to safeguard biodiversity, both concepts in reality tie local communities into a development vision limited by both a reliance on the natural environment and the limited development perspective of sustainability. This partial and degraded sense of development is of no long-term benefit to local communities. There is nothing essentially wrong in local communities benefiting from revenues accrued through foreign visitors, but to see this as the means by which local communities develop, whilst at the same time restricting any attempts they may have to transform their real social position, is nothing more than enforcing primitivism.

AFTERWORD

Tiffany Jenkins

The essays in this book leave the reader in no doubt that debating what holidays and travelling are for, and how these activities should be carried out, highlights just how much travel is changing. Going on holiday is no longer an uncontentious activity, and many programmes and policies have been developed to shape and change how we travel. The concept 'responsible (or ethical) tourism' is at the centre of these changes. But who benefits from responsible tourism? Contributors to this book have disagreed about both whether those who travel, and the countries they travel to, gain from this approach to travel.

THE TRAVELLER

'RESPONSIBLE TOURISM' IS A BOON FOR THE TRAVELLER

Advocates of responsible tourism make the case that travellers and tourists benefit because their holiday or trip is greatly enhanced by this approach to travel. If those who travel have made the effort to find out more about the host country and its people, they will understand it better and get more out of the visit. Travelling will therefore provide more fascinating and enriching experiences for the tourist through meaningful encounters with local people and an appreciation of cultural matters and the environment than it otherwise would. Some advocates of responsible tourism explain that where this approach is adopted, the time spent in the country is more 'authentic' and 'real' than it would otherwise be, as travellers come to understand the local culture better. Going to another country is less a holiday and more an experience and this, the advocates of responsible travel claim, is what more and more people want.

However, some supporters of this kind of tourism caution against travellers believing that prior knowledge about their destination is enough. Rather, they argue, there is a danger that travellers absolve themselves of the responsibility that travelling involves, by believing that their action in going to another country has consequences only for them. Those who have these concerns argue that knowledge is not enough and that travellers should be actively ethical in the host country.

RESPONSIBLE TOURISM RESTRICTS AND PATRONIZES HOLIDAYMAKERS

Critics of the ethos of ethical tourism argue, in contrast, that it greatly restricts and even ruins the experience of travel. Those who argue this viewpoint take issue with the assumption that codes and guidelines that aim to make tourists responsible are either necessary or effective. Much of the time such codes are blanket prescriptions for situations that are not that straightforward and therefore cannot really be applied wherever and whenever, they contend. In some cases, such codes could even be wrong and inappropriate. It is really only travellers who can use their judgement effectively in a particular situation and they have to be trusted to do so.

Some critics suggest additionally that such codes are not only unhelpful, but are not what they appear. They aim more to regulate the tourist than benefit the host country. Such concern about the behaviour of those who travel is worrying, it is claimed, since an attitude that deems it necessary to monitor and advise people about how to behave shackles the spirit of adventure where the individual is free and is encouraged to experiment and explore. Codes of conduct position those who promote ethical travel as the parent to a small child. They are not necessary for grown adults and are also patronizing and damaging.

Some critics go further and argue that ethical tourism implies snobbishness that looks down on the average person. Advocates of ethical tourism have turned going on holiday into a moral exercise it is claimed, and by moralizing travel, they have problematized the fun, freedom and luxury that many people seek as 'bad behaviour'. The message of ethical tourism advocates is that those that travel without an 'ethical' mindset are crude, cheap and common – a mindset that reflects a true disillusionment with the majority of people. Some suggest that ethical tourism carries a similar message to that of the Victorian moralizers and missionaries. Ethical tourism may have the language of ethics and responsibility but it is really about restricting travel for the masses and keeping it for the privileged, 'moral' few, and it implies that those who are not ethical should not really be allowed to travel.

Some opponents of ethical tourism also argue that codes and guidelines make relations worse between people from different countries. They suggest that the ethical tourism industry perpetuates the idea that people are defined by their differences and cannot understand each other. Criticism of this kind contends that the elevated concept of 'culture' that ethical tourists promote is a fetishized and imposed notion that both exaggerates differences between travellers and locals and idealizes and degrades local people. This, the detractors of ethical travel argue, hampers the ability for locals and tourists to get to know and understand each other. Too many codes of conduct, and explanations of how different local people are from those from other countries, make it harder for people to relate to each other. If people are just left to travel as they see fit, they are more likely to make links and have conversations that are spontaneous and less controlled, and thus communicate with and understand others more, not less.

LOCALS AND THEIR COUNTRIES

RESPONSIBLE TRAVEL IS A BENEFIT FOR LOCALS AND THEIR COUNTRIES

Those who promote ethical tourism believe it can improve life for local people. Unlike 'normal' holidaymakers, when ethical tourists visit a country they act wisely and bring benefit. For example, visitors can spend money in the village and not in a big hotel thus ensuring the locals get the much-needed money, rather than it going to a large company. Ethical tourists will also take account of poverty by opting not to haggle in a situation where the difference of a few pennies to them is inconsiderable, but could mean a lot to the local selling goods in the market. This approach contends that even minor changes in the behaviour of tourists can bring great benefits to the host country.

However, there is more to being an ethical tourist, maintain its supporters. Travellers can make very important contributions to the conservation of the natural environment. Through supporting wildlife parks and shunning overdeveloped areas, responsible travellers can ensure that natural beauty and, in some cases, wilderness areas are not destroyed. By respecting the diversity of the animal kingdom and the natural world, responsible tourists can be careful to ensure that these areas are not ruined. Areas free from industry and development are thus not destroyed in the name of holidaymaking.

Ethical tourists who respect the culture of the host county can also help conserve the cultural heritage, it is claimed. We should respect the differences and way of life of the people and help maintain it. The ethical tourist who is culturally sensitive engenders respect between tourists and hosts, unlike the tourist who has no knowledge of the local people and how they live.

ETHICAL TOURISM IS A NEW IMPERIALISM

Opponents of ethical tourism contend, in contrast, that an idea about what is good for the host country is imposed by its advocates, which overrides the choices and decisions of the locals. Critics argue that this imposition means that in fact *ethical tourists* decide what is right for the host country and that this is highly problematic. They contend that there is a particular outlook held by supporters of ethical tourism, which prioritizes nature over development, and upholds a romanticized ideal of culture, over the host country's view of their best interests. Nature and the environment are held to be so important by the ethical tourist that locals are shunted and shoved around and are treated as less important than wildlife and wilderness. Ethical tourists disregard what locals really want and need; there is no equal collaboration. The impulse to conserve means that the host country is instructed on what to do and how to behave on the basis of what is good for the Western tourist looking for a romantic sanctuary. Local people are consequently expelled from their land and there is increased regulation of their lives.

Critics of ethical travel claim that the ethical tourist searches for their idea of the local culture which overrides the reality of the local culture and locals' interests. The ethical tourist is so keen to find their idealized native, for example, that they enforce a situation that creates and maintains their vision. They only support the happy primitive that suits their needs as tourists in search of an 'experience'. This is oppressive and backward, it is argued. Therefore the host country and its people do not benefit from ethical tourism.

The benefits and drawbacks of ethical tourism will continue to be discussed and debated. We hope that the essays in this book have helped to elucidate the beliefs and tensions in the debate and go some way to explain the assumptions and ideas that lie behind the answers to the question: Who benefits from ethical tourism?

If you have found this book interesting, and agree that 'debating matters', you can find out more about the Institute of Ideas and our programme of live conferences and debates by visiting our website **www.instituteofideas.com**.
Alternatively you can email **info@instituteofideas.com**
or call 020 7269 9220 to receive a full programme of events and information about joining the Institute of Ideas.

Other titles available in this series:

DEBATING MATTERS

Institute of Ideas
Expanding the Boundaries of Public Debate

ANIMAL EXPERIMENTATION:

GOOD OR BAD?

Some argue that animal experiments are vital to advance scientific knowledge and improve medical practice. Others believe that they are unnecessary, cruel and repetitive. Do animals experience pain and suffering in the same ways as humans; if so should they be given rights? Is a compromise between animal rights campaigners and those who emphasize the needs of humans possible or even desirable?

Key figures in the debate exchange their views on this contentious issue:

- Dr Stuart Derbyshire, scientist at the University of Pittsburgh, US, researching central mechanisms of pain
- Dr Mark Matfield, medical research scientist
- Dr Tom Regan, Professor of Philosophy and President of The Culture & Animals Foundation
- Dr Richard D. Ryder, author of *Painism: a Modern Morality.*

ABORTION:

Currently around 180 000 British women terminate pregnancies each year – far more than the politicians who passed the Abortion Act in 1967 intended. Should the law be made more liberal to reflect demand for abortion? Is the problem that in Britain, women still do not have the 'right to choose'? Or is it too easy for women to 'take the life' of their 'unborn children'? What role should doctors play in the abortion decision?

Contrasting answers are presented in this book by:

- Ann Furedi, director of communications, British Pregnancy Advisory Service
- Mary Kenny, journalist and writer
- Theodore Darymple, GP and author of *Mass Listeria: The Meaning of Health Scares* and *An Intelligent Person's Guide to Medicine*.
- Emily Jackson, Lecturer in Law, London School of Economics
- Helen Watt, director, Linacre Centre for Healthcare Ethics.

REALITY TV:

HOW REAL IS REAL?

What is reality TV, and how real is it anyway? From gameshows such as *Big Brother* to docusoaps and even history programmes, television seems to be turning its attentions onto 'real people'. Does this mean that television is becoming more democratic, or is reality TV a fad that has had its day? Does reality TV reflect society as it really is, or merely manufacture disposable celebrities?

Contrasting views come from:

- Christopher Dunkley, television critic for the *Financial Times*
- Dr Graham Barnfield, Lecturer in Journalism, The Surrey Institute of Art & Design
- Victoria Mapplebeck, TV producer of the TV shows *Smart Hearts* and *Meet the Kilshaws*
- Bernard Clark, documentary maker.

NATURE'S REVENGE?

Politicians and the media rarely miss the opportunity that hurricanes or extensive flooding provide to warn us of the potential dangers of global warming. This is nature's 'wake-up call' we are told and we must adjust our lifestyles.

This book brings together scientific experts and social commentators to debate whether we really are seeing 'nature's revenge':

- Dr Mike Hulme, Executive Director of the Tyndall Centre for Climate Change Research
- Julian Morris, Director of International Policy Network
- Professor Peter Sammonds, who researches natural hazards at University College London
- Charles Secrett, Executive Director of Friends of the Earth.

SCIENCE:

CAN WE TRUST THE EXPERTS?

Controversies surrounding a plethora of issues, from the MMR vaccine to mobile phones, from BSE to genetically-modified foods, have led many to ask how the public's faith in government advice can be restored. At the heart of the matter is the role of the expert and the question of whose opinion to trust.

In this book, prominent participants in the debate tell us their views:

- Bill Durodié, who researches risk and precaution at New College, Oxford University
- Dr Ian Gibson MP, Chairman of thc Parliamentary Offlce of Science and Technology
- Dr Sue Mayer, Executive Director of Genewatch UK
- Dr Doug Parr, Chief Scientist for Greenpeace UK.

COMPENSATION CRAZY:

DO WE BLAME AND CLAIM TOO MUCH?

Big compensation pay-outs make the headlines. New style 'claims centres' advertise for accident victims promising 'where there's blame, there's a claim'. Many commentators fear Britain is experiencing a US-style compensation craze. But what's wrong with holding employers and businesses to account? Or are we now too ready to reach for our lawyers and to find someone to blame when things go wrong?

These questions and more are discussed by:

- Ian Walker, personal injury litigator
- Tracey Brown, risk analyst
- John Peysner, Professor of civil litigation
- Daniel Lloyd, lawyer.